S U R

FOLK
TALES

SURREY

FOLK TALES

JANET DOWLING

ILLUSTRATED BY

LAWRENCE HEATH

The
History
Press

To the memory of my uncle, Alick Anderson, who was the first storyteller who sparked in me a love of stories. As a six-year-old child I sat at his feet while he regaled us with tales of his adventures travelling the world, honouring the folk tales from Australia, New Zealand and the North Americas.

First published 2013

The History Press
The Mill, Brimscombe Port
Stroud, Gloucestershire, GL5 2QG
www.thehistorypress.co.uk

British Library Cataloguing in Publication Data.
A catalogue record for this book is available from the British Library.

ISBN 978 0 7524 6635 4

Typesetting and origination by The History Press
Printed in Great Britain

CONTENTS

ACKNOWLEDGEMENTS

Many thanks to Kathy McClenaghan, Linda Day, Raewyn Bloomfield and Lucy Phelps for coming with me across the Surrey landscapes looking for dragons, giants, witches, and smugglers, as well as murdered men and women.

Many thanks to Mathew Alexander, John Janeway, W.H. Chouler and Eric Parker, who all trawled the primary sources before me and published their own versions of the folk tale material.

Thanks also to Jeremy Harte who, in his own trawling of the Surrey archives, was happy to spot odd bits of Surrey folklore and legend and share them with me, even if he didn't quite approve of what I did with them, thus maintaining the age-old tension between what a folklorist records and a storyteller retells! Thanks to Alan Moore, Juliette Chaplin and David Rose, who also shared their notes and information. To Irene Shuttle who shared her experience of Surrey folk songs, and to the staff at Halsway Manor who found me a Ruth Tongue story. And to Richard Wood, who helped me when a couple of tales refused to be written.

Many thanks to Lucy and Guy Phelps, Jean and Merv McGee, June Woodward, Margaret Ball, Kim Marks, Samantha Johnson, Robbie and Evan Artro-Morris. They are all from the Chestnut Avenue Book Club, and read and gave feedback on my penultimate drafts; I would also like to thank their children, Nell, Freya, Bella, Karin and Liam, who listened to the child-friendly versions of the tales and gave me good feedback. Plus the newest member of the Chestnut clan – young Megan – who will grow up knowing some of these tales because her mother travelled on the journey with me. This book is dedicated to all six of them, and the children in the schools where I have told these tales. But parents beware – like all folk tales, you need to adapt a story to the ear of the listener or the eye of the reader.

Many thanks to the audience of the Three Heads in a Well storytelling club in Ewell and the members of the Surrey Storytellers Guild, who listened to me telling and retelling the adult versions of the tales. They told me what worked well, and how the stories could be even better if …

Thanks to Lawrence Heath for drawing such divine silhouette illustrations (at the same time as supporting his son Liam successfully prepare for kayaking in the Olympics).

Many thanks to Dianne Symons, Joan Roberts and Fran Andrews for proofreading and challenging me on my grammar, and to Hannah Gosden for her help with The Wild Cherry Tree and the Nuthatch.

And finally, thanks to my long-suffering husband, Jeff Ridge, who supports me in all I do, who also went dragon hunting and searching in caves with me, who drew the map of the stories, and who coped with the writing at midnight and the wringing of hands when all seemed doom, gloom and despondency.

INTRODUCTION

These are the folk tales of Surrey. But what kind of Surrey, you might ask?

Surrey used to be a lot bigger. Before 1889 it extended as far north as the Thames and as far east as Rotherhithe. In 1889, the London boroughs of Lambeth, Southwark and Wandsworth were created and removed from Surrey, and Croydon was made into a county borough. In 1928, Addington moved over to Croydon, and in 1965 Surrey lost more land with the creation of the London boroughs of Kingston, Richmond, Merton and Sutton. Most of these areas retain Surrey as part of their postal address today.

So, back to the question – what kind of Surrey? Conferring with the author of *London Folk Tales*, it became apparent that she was using the old definition of London and that the South London boroughs might be disenfranchised from representation because they fell between two stools! Thus most of these folk tales come from within the modern-day boundary of Surrey, and four come from the pre-1889 boundary.

Writing a book of the folk tales from your local community is always going to be a challenging journey, and there is a difference between an area you have known as a child and one you enter as an adult. I grew up in the East End of London, and know many stories about that locality. Some are true, some not so true, some are definitely lost in myth and some we might have made up and forgotten that we did so. So it is interesting to come to an area as an adult and look for the traditional stories. But who should you ask, and where?

I have now lived in Surrey for twenty years, and when I asked people what stories they grew up with, they knew very few, and most often told me about the Silent Pool. You will find that one in this book under the legend of Stephan Langton, along with the circumstances under which it was written and the influence it has had on the local appreciation of folk tales. But that was it. Even the members of the Chestnut Avenue Book Club, most of whom had grown up and lived in Surrey, did not know of any folk tales. Indeed, the story of Mathew Trigg and the Pharisees was a complete revelation to the two members who came from Ash, even though the action took place in their hometown.

So where do stories go when they are not being told? This year is the 200th anniversary of the first publication of the Brothers Grimm collection of folk tales. Their first compilation consisted of German folk tales, designed to help German lawyers understand the underpinning values of the law in all the disparate principalities that made the German people. When it became clear that their best-selling market was families, they began collecting more stories, but this time they were not so fussy about where the stories came from originally. So they were happy to collect from their French Huguenot friends, and other stories from around Europe. Furthermore, they trimmed the stories to suit a family audience. They took out some of the sex, cranked up some of the violence (if you were bad, then really bad things happened to you), and then tidied up some of the stories so that they fitted a set structure. In some cases, they completely rewrote them. What started as a faithful reporting of tales as they were told, then became a creative rewriting exercise with intrinsic values introduced and reinforced. How much of this process did I dare replicate? How much should I avoid? I decided that I would have one underlying value – that whatever was told as a Surrey folk tale would have to come from a piece of folklore that was rooted in Surrey. Then I would have to see what happened, but I would be faithful to my source.

So I ask again, where do stories go when they are not being told? They are occasionally recorded in travellers' writings and old histories of the county – so Aubrey, Cobbett, and Manning and Bray refer to some. I have been fortunate in that local historians like Mathew Alexander, John Janeway, Eric Parker and W.H. Chouler had all published their own reports of the folk tale material. When you know that a tale exists about a particular area, it is much easier to start researching than when you know nothing at all!

As I trawled through the original sources myself, I began to despair about finding something that hadn't already been collected – they had all been so diligent and comprehensive. But on the other hand, I realised that I would be bringing my skill as a storyteller to the stories – which is why you might find some of my retellings different to how they are reported in the collections of historians and folklorists. Be assured that I have found the original sources, drawn on them, and not wandered too far away! But some of the dilemmas faced by the Grimms suddenly opened up before me, and I could see myself potentially falling into the same traps that they did. The folklorists and historians of Surrey might not be too happy with me. One folklorist provided me with some material about the field names in Titsey Wood and a piece of local folklore. I mixed it with some information about the Site of Special Scientific Interest, and the folklore of the plants found there, to create the story told here. Shall we say that his face was a picture when I retold the story at Three Heads in a Well story club!

Sometimes the stories, like 'The Dragon of West Clandon', were well established. I originally knew the story from Alexander's recounting of it, and I found the original newspaper article which described the solder killing the 'serpent' (later known as the dragon), which placed the story in history rather than legend. However, I remained curious to know why he was described as a deserter. I was quite astonished to discover the revolt which forms the first part of the story, which is all true and based on contemporary events which occurred just a year before the newspaper report.

Sometimes I found hints of stories – perhaps just one line. 'A dish fit for a queen' is an example of one, where the research brought up a line that said William the Conqueror had assigned to his chef, Tezelin, the manor of Addington, and that the holder of the manor should present a certain dish to the monarch at the coronation. That was all that was said, but in the retelling the rest just fell into place.

Sometimes it was tempting to make up a story. For example, the Hogs Back is a stunning feature in Surrey, and with a name like the Hogs Back there must surely be a story behind it. Even Jane Austen refers to it! But alas, the answer is simply that the expression 'Hogs Back' is a geological term to describe a narrow ridge with steeply inclined slopes. Reader, you will find no made-up stories about hogs.

Several years ago I did a project for the Surrey Hills Board, collecting and retelling local folk tales that were suitable for a family audience. The results are at http://www.surreyhills.org/surrey-hills-explore/tales-of-surrey-hills. You will recognise some of these tales here too, but if you compare them you will also notice that the language, and sometimes the content, is different. That's because I have been telling and retelling the stories in my work with local schools and communities, and, as I have told them, they have developed their own character. I deliberately did not revisit the stories on the Surrey Hills website until I had written my current version of the tales. You may be interested to have a look, to see how much some of them have developed and how much some of them have remained untouched. This is my equivalent of having a first edition and subsequent editions for comparison.

However, there are two stories that I do put my hand up to introducing. I adapted a Chinese tale to explain the presence of the Surrey puma, and my rationale for its inclusion is that I have been telling it for so long in local schools that it has probably made its way into local folklore. And several years ago I deliberately made up another story to show local schools how a true-life event might become a folk tale. I have included it in this collection as it actually came back to me, and was the only story I 'collected' from a chance encounter in a café!

There are, I am sure, many more stories out there. In my research notes I have hints of countless more. Alas, my calls to newspapers went unheeded, as I tried to invite people to share their stories. Maybe with this publication, people might be inspired to retell their own tales as well as reclaiming these stories. I invite them to contact me at JanetTells@gmail.com.

Some storytellers in this series have numbered the stories in sequence; some have grouped them into common themes, or grouped them so that they reflect the nature of the landscape. I have chosen to put them in a sequence that follows a route around the county, starting and returning to almost the same place. On a sunny weekend you could do your own Story Bike Tour of Surrey!

Janet Dowling, 2013

Numbers on this map identify the general location
of the tales and the chapter in this book

ONE

THE DRAGON OF
WEST CLANDON

If you drive down the A426, you might just see an outline of a dragon on the local embankment, at the West Clandon crossroads. Be careful, as it can only be seen from the road going westbound to Guildford, and it might be grassed over. But it's one of a cluster of dragons that Surrey has to offer!

Look there! Can you see? It's a soldier, on the run in his own country. He looks close to collapsing. He's as thin as a rake and is scavenging to find something to eat, to fill his belly.

The war with Napoleon was going badly. England hadn't been prepared for a war so close to its own shores and men were hurriedly recruited to join the army and navy, as well as the local militia. There was hardly any training, and with poor leadership they were sent to fight in France and the Lowlands. When the military expedition to the Lowlands failed miserably, and was followed by the evacuation back to England, the morale of the men was at its lowest. Packed in their barracks at Blatchingford, there was little privacy and, due to the poor harvest, food and provisions were limited. The men were hungry, and 500 of them marched to Newhaven to take the town and find food to fill their bellies. The officers persuaded some of them to return to the barracks, but many stayed in the town and the Dragoons were called out to bring them back. Some men escaped into the countryside, but the men who remained were caught, court-martialled then whipped, transported, or even shot in front of a firing squad.

And that's how we find the soldier of our story. Cold and wet. Running from his own troops. He knew that he faced a court-martial and possible death, after all he had done for his country. His only thought was to return to his family, possibly for one last time. The only clothes on his back were his uniform, which marked him out as a deserter. He muddied them as best he could to disguise himself, but only succeeded in making himself look more frightening. He had to live on what he could find on the land, as he made his way home.

He slept in ditches and under bushes. He didn't know the lie of the land, and had to make his best guess, knowing that his home was somewhere north-west. As long as he could see the sun, he could get his bearings. He wasn't a coward, but he had had enough of the disrespect that was given to a man who fought for his country, and was not given the dignity of food. But now, after two days on the roads, hiding from every passer-by, coach and horseman, he had even less to eat. Berries and nuts do little to fill a man's stomach. He kept a lookout for isolated cottages, hoping to beg for food there.

His attention was caught by a dog barking ahead of him. He came to a clearing and saw a cottage there. A woman came out with a basket of scraps and threw them to one side. Amongst them he could see a bone with meat on. With no thought except his belly, he scrambled forward to get it, but was beaten by a dog that picked up the bone and ran off. With whatever strength he had left, the soldier was now fixated on that bone and chased the dog. The bone fell from the dog's mouth, and he stopped to pick it up again. This was the soldier's chance, and he threw himself on the dog, grasping the bone. There followed a tussle between them, neither prepared to let go, until the soldier suddenly realised what he was doing. He fell to his knees and gave a great wail of despair. Part of him wondered if he would have been better off being whipped, transported or shot.

As the sobs wracked his body, he became aware of a warm wetness on his hand. The dog had placed the bone in front of him, and was licking his hand. The first act of kindness he had experienced in a long time had come from a dog.

The dog stayed; it snuggled beside him at night to keep warm and was a companion during the day. It didn't take much for the soldier to feel that the dog was his dearest friend and a fine hunting partner for catching the odd rabbit to roast on a fire.

Alas, that's how he was discovered. The smoke attracted attention and men from the local militia found him. He ran as fast as he could, the dog beside him barking. He was overwhelmed; the militia kicked at the dog and one of them took a club to him.

The soldier was taken to the local lock-up, to be returned to his unit and court-martialled. He knew that his desertion meant he faced certain death by firing squad. His only thought now was for his dog. But no one could tell him where it had gone. There was no rush to move the soldier back. Paperwork had to be done, escorts had to be arranged. It all took time.

While he was in the lock-up he heard a story. A serpent – a dragon – was threatening the people of West Clandon. A huge thing that would block the path, and take small animals. The people were afraid to walk out in the day, let alone at night. Mothers kept their children indoors, and both men and women walked cautiously, afraid to disturb the dragon. Life was greatly disrupted, and yet no one was brave enough to face up to the creature.

Perhaps here was a chance to redeem himself. The soldier sent a message to the local magistrates, saying that he would attempt to kill the dragon – in exchange for a pardon if he was successful. It was an unusual request, but on the other hand, it's not as though you have a dragon threatening the local community every day.

It was agreed. If he killed the dragon they would make representations for his pardon, for services to the community. They agreed to give him a rifle with a bayonet – but no ammunition. When they let him out of the lock-up, he blinked in the sunshine. He was taken to West Clandon and allowed to go. He was warned that the militia was standing by, and if he tried to escape before fulfilling his end of the bargain, they would hunt him down and shoot him.

How do you look for a dragon? Do you call it? How do you summon it? How do you stalk it? He looked around for evidence of a dragon, going from field to field, sniffing the air. He finally found some pellets on the ground that he didn't recognise. Could this be dragon spoor? Whatever it was, it was fresh. He was in a field called Deadacre. The field was quite large, and no crops were growing this year. There were several grassy mounds. One mound was particularly large and not quite like the others.

He approached it, and was suddenly aware of an eye in the knoll, that just opened and stared at him. The soldier shook himself, no time to wonder, no time to be mesmerised; this was a time to kill the beast!

He charged with his bayonet, ready to strike, and that's when the dragon uncurled itself and rose to its full height, towering over the soldier. It had long claws, teeth that were yellow and sharp, and a long spiky tail that unfurled. The soldier suddenly realised that this might not be so easy, but he stood his ground. He was no coward.

He lunged and lunged again at the dragon, but his bayonet seemed to just bounce off the dragon's skin. The dragon was lashing at him with its claws, and it caught the soldier's cheek. The pain was so intense that the soldier thought he would faint, but still he stood his ground. Lunge, thrust. Lunge, thrust. Lunge, thrust.

The dragon now towered over him, its yellow teeth dripping with poisoned saliva; one bite could be fatal. The solder thought he was going to die.

Suddenly there was a sound behind him that could make even hell turn over – but he didn't dare take his eyes from the dragon. Something flew from the side of the field, almost over his shoulder,

and fastened itself onto the neck of the dragon. The force of the attack was so great that the dragon tumbled to the ground, and was secured by the weight of its nemesis. The soldier could now see the place where the dragon's heart was beating just under the skin, allowing him to thrust his bayonet in with all of his might.

There was a soul-curdling cry from the dragon, a shuddering of the torso, and a final lash from the tail. The dragon was dead.

Then another noise. Barking! Still gripping the neck of the dragon was a dog. His dog. His companion. The dog let go and then jumped up at the soldier, greeting him with the joy of a long-lost friend. And they both fell to the ground, laughing and barking.

The soldier was pardoned and the people of West Clandon thanked him for his help. We don't know if the soldier went back into the army, or whether he did go home, but to commemorate the battle with the dragon a wooden plaque was commissioned that was held in the local parsonage for everyone to see.

Sadly the plaque was stolen, but the people of West Clandon have long memories. A new one was made and is now kept in the Church of St Peter and St Paul. As you go into the church through the north door, just look up and you will see it there.

TWO

ST MARTHA AND
THE DRAGON

Outside Guildford there is a hill, and at the top of the hill is the most delightful chapel of St Martha. In the evening sun it is a glorious sight, and one of the most beautiful settings in the Surrey Hills. In the winter snow, it stands out and has a promise of comfort for those who make the steep climb to the top. Inside is a standard with St Martha ... and a dragon!

A long time ago, St Martha, her sister Mary Magdalene and her brother Lazarus were expelled from the Holy Land, the land of their birth, and sent into the sea in a boat with no sails, no oars and no rudder. They were at the mercy of the sea and the sea monsters. They had no control over where they were taken, or which shore they would be washed up on. Their faith was in the hands of their god and their master, as they were disciples of Jesus Christ.

They finally landed in the south of the place we now know as France, at St Marie de la Mer. It was AD 48 and Martha was preaching the word of the Christian god. She travelled to Aix, and the people there were so impressed by her words that they converted to Christianity. One man tried to hear her from the other side of the River Rhone. Frustrated, he dived into the waters and attempted to swim across, but the current was so strong that he was swept away. His lifeless body was found the next day and brought before Martha. She spoke the words of her god and life was restored to him. She was a powerful and able speaker.

But Martha was not the only one to have been expelled from their homeland. A beast, half-animal and half-fish, had been spurned in its birthplace of Galicia, Turkey. Now it wandered the highways, byways and waterways, trying to find a place to call home. It was a Tarascus, the offspring of the great sea serpent called the Leviathan, and the great snake Bonacho. It was greater than an ox and longer than a horse; it had teeth as sharp as a sword, horns on either side of its head, the head of a lion and a tail like a serpent. At home both on water and land, it took what it needed to survive. And if that was a man, woman or child, then all the more for its belly. No one was safe: boats were crushed, carts were wrecked, and horses, cows and sheep were all devoured.

Eventually the Tarascus settled in a place called Nerluc between Avignon and Arles. Perhaps the climate suited it. Perhaps it had good access to both land and water. Perhaps it was just tired of forever wandering. But the people of Nerluc lived in fear and despair. They could not risk tilling their fields and they could not risk caring for their animals. They tried hard enough to hunt it down, and great gangs of men would try to surround it. But when pursued, the Tarascus would let go a pile of dung from its bowels and flood the area; anyone who came into contact with it experienced a burning sensation and became incapacitated. Just right for an aromatic meal for the Tarascus.

The people of Nerluc offered a reward to anyone who could rid them of this demon. There were many men who tried, but no one survived long enough to claim it. Then they heard of the miracles that Martha was performing and they sent messengers to ask her to help them. They were not sure what to expect. Perhaps they thought she would arrive with an army. Perhaps they thought she had the ear of a god that would strike the Tarascus down with lightning. What they did not expect was a woman in a white dress and no shoes, who carried nothing but a cross and holy water, and wore a girdle.

The people of Nerluc were shocked and dismayed. They had put all their hopes into a miracle happening, and did not believe that this woman would be able to do anything. They started arguing amongst themselves about who was to blame, and some of the men started fighting. Martha shook her head. She understood that they were just afraid, and also ashamed that they could not protect their families, even though the situation was beyond their control. She left them behind her, arguing still, as she walked into the woods surrounding the village.

The first thing she noticed was the smell. The Tarascus had been generous with its dung donations, and she idly wondered how the undergrowth would grow back the next year. The ground underfoot was very boggy, and she didn't want to think any more about what she might be walking on. The air had a bitter taste to it, and she could imagine the burning sensation that would come from too much exposure to it. But the overwhelming thing that she noticed was the complete lack of sound. Not a bird sang; not a leaf rustled with the movement of a mouse, rabbit or snake. There was no life at all, apart from the butterflies, newly emerged, looking for the nectar which they needed to survive.

In the distance she heard a shout, then a scream. A traveller on the road had met his end. She made her way in the same direction.

She found the Tarascus devouring its prey. Yes, it was a man, and as the Tarascus tore into the body to eat the flesh, the head fell off and rolled to Martha's feet. A look of terror was fixed on the face. For a moment Martha hesitated, thinking of the pain of the man who had died. Then, sending up a prayer for forgiveness to her god, Martha picked the head up and walked towards the Tarascus with it in her hands. The blood dripped from the jaws of the monster as it looked up, startled.

She could see the confusion in its eyes as she stood there. This
didn't make sense to the beast. This prey should be running from
it, rather than proffering the head as more food. Prey that ran was
tenderer to eat.

Martha took advantage of those precious seconds of uncer-
tainty. She took out her bottle of holy water and splashed it
around the Tarascus. Initially it roared as if the drops burned it,
as its own dung did to others. But she let go of the head she
carried, letting it roll towards the Tarascus, to shift its attention.
Then she took her cross and placed it in front of the beast's eyes,
moving it from side to side as she called upon her god to bring
salvation to the Tarascus.

An almighty roar came out of the beast, then it stretched up
in the air, as though it was in a struggle with some unknown
entity, and finally it sat back down on the ground, exhausted, its
head in obeisance to Martha. She took the girdle from around
her waist and tied it around its neck. She gave a small tug, and
the Tarascus rose to its feet; it then followed her, meek and
docile, like a lamb.

The villagers were still arguing loudly as she returned, but first
one then another saw Martha and her companion. They could
not believe what they saw. The Tarascus in their village! Staves,
knives, swords and clubs – anything that could give a blow was
used to beat the Tarascus to death. Martha pleaded with them,
saying that the monster was now tamed, but the villagers declared

that it must be put to death as punishment for its wickedness. When it was all over, and the body lay on the ground, battered and broken, they realised what they had done. They were confused and uncertain. Protection had been their focus, but the beast had been rendered defenceless before them. They had their miracle release, but at what price for their souls?

⚭

The villagers still debate today whether or not they were right to kill the beast. But since 1474 they have held a festival which celebrates the coming of St Martha to release them from the tyranny of the Tarascus. They even changed the name of the town to Tarascon to remember it and the deed they performed. You can visit the place at festival time and see a Tarascus parading the streets – until St Martha uses the holy water and cross to soothe it, and her girdle to bring it back home.

⚭

And there are some people who will tell you that there was another miracle that day. When the body of the Tarascus was dumped far away from the village, Martha went to find it, and restored it to life. It then became her devoted servant and protector, and travelled with her on her journeys. And some people will even tell you that she came to England with the Tarascus, and to Guildford itself, where she founded the chapel on top of St Martha's Hill and lived out her days. Some people will tell you that the Tarascus stayed with her all of her days, and that when she died, the Tarascus died too. The local people buried him in the ground near St Martha's Church, and over time the mound became a hill, and became known as Dragon or Draco Hill and eventually Drake's Hill. Nowadays we call it St Catherine's Hill. There used to be a holy well there that had healing powers, and some people would tell you that the well was really the tears of the dragon. Some people could tell you that, but I can't possibly say!

🐊

⣎⣀⣹

St Catherine's Hill has been cut through for the A3100 road out of Guildford. You can see the remnants of the stream of dragon tears along the side of the park and ride at Artington.

THREE

HOW THE GIANT SISTERS LEARNED ABOUT COOPERATION

There are variants of this story in other parts of England.

⊙⊃⊂⊙

Once upon a time there were two sisters. They did everything together, and nothing together, because whatever they were doing they were in competition with each other. Each one wanted to be the greatest and the best. And if you are keeping an eye on what the other is doing, you are not doing your best. So if one was baking a cake, then the other would be trying to do the same. Except that one would end up putting too much salt in, and the other would forget the sugar. If one was trying to chop down a tree, the other would join in. Have you ever tried to chop down a tree with two people chopping in different directions, each trying to be the first to get it to fall and cry 'Timber!'? It just doesn't work, and is more likely to be dangerous for someone else!

For most people this would be a sorry state of affairs, but these were no ordinary sisters. They were giants. And I don't mean 6ft-tall giants, but giants that are as tall as the trees. When giants make mistakes, everything comes crashing down around them, and it's the little people like you and me that generally end up having to sort it all out.

But one day they met a man who told them the most amazing stories. Stories about people who helped each other. People who cared for their neighbours and even strangers. People who thought about others, before they thought about themselves. These two sisters were astounded that anyone would want to actually help another person. They had always been taught that they had to be the top giant, and to hell with anyone else or the consequences. They were particularly touched by the story of a man who was left on the wayside for dead. People he thought were his friends passed him by; it was a stranger who found him and cared for him. The two sisters were so impressed by the stories that they wanted to know more, and that is how they became Christians. They calmed down a lot, and became politer and friendlier towards each other and the people in the local villages.

With this new-found faith, and a new-found way of thinking, they wanted to express their thanks by building chapels just outside Guildford: one on St Catherine's Hill, the other on St Martha's Hill. That way the sun could shine on the righteous and the right house at the same time!

There was one problem: they only had one hammer between them! They were sure that they owned one each – where was the other one? Maybe the other giants had hidden it for protection. Maybe, when there had been some jealousy between the two sisters, one had hidden the other's hammer. But either way, neither of them could remember where the second hammer was. Once upon a time it would have been a scramble to get the hammer first. But now it was different!

'You have it first.'

'No, you have it first.'

'I insist. You have it first.'

'No no, you take it.'

This could have gone on for days, weeks, months, and even years – nothing would ever get built. What were they to do? The wise old woman (because there is always a wise old woman) shook her head. She called both of the giant sisters to her, and whispered to them.

'Of course!' Both sisters cried in unison, 'That's the obvious way to do it.'

They both looked at the hammer, still waiting for the other to pick it up. The wise old woman raised her eyes to the sky, and muttered to them while waving her finger about. I don't know what she said, but it may have been something like: 'Up scout, walk out.'

She pointed to one of the sisters, who then picked up the hammer and bounded to her chosen hill. The wood was set up, the nail put in place, and then 'thunk'. The nail was well and truly hammered. Then she turned, and, seeing her sister ready on the far side, called out, 'Sister!' With all of her strength she threw the hammer to the other hill, where the sister caught it fast. She set her wood, placed her nail, and 'Thunk'. Then she turned and called out, 'Sister!' Now with all of *her* strength she threw the hammer to the other hill, where the sister caught it fast. She set her wood, placed her nail, and 'Thunk'.

And that's how they shared the hammer, sending it back and forth. All day long. And as the sun went down, they had each gone as far as the other in building their chapels. That's the way sisters work together!

❦

The sister hills of St Martha and St Catherine are still there – one with a church on top that is still alive and vibrant, the other with the ruins of on old priory. In the setting sun, especially in the autumn when the light begins to turn, they are both fabulous views to see from a distance.

FOUR

HOW THE POWER OF A DREAM AND A PIKE CREATED A GREAT MAN

As you walk through the High Street in Guildford, you will see the River Wey at the bottom of the hill. There's a bridge over it and you can stand there in all weathers, trying to spot the fish. They seem to hover in the water, with the water washing over them, apparently in a struggle upstream and yet going nowhere. Every now and then, one of them darts away and finds a different place to linger. You can see chubb, roach, and even some gudgeon. If you are very lucky you might even see a pike, the scourge of the rest of the fish, and one that local fishermen would like to catch. Nobody is sure if there are any pike left in the stream, but there was certainly one once. A big one. And no matter how many tried, nobody could catch it.

In the town lived Maurice Abbot and his wife Alice. He was a cloth maker starting out in business, while his wife was expecting another child: such excitement and anticipation for them both! Maurice was anxious about whether he could do good enough business to be able to look after his growing family. Alice gave him all the reassurance he needed, but she was concerned too.

One night she had a dream. It was as if an angel had spoken to her about all her worries. Just as she had reassured Maurice, so the voice reassured her that her son would be a fine and strong lad, and if Alice could only eat the pike in the River Wey, then she could be certain that he would become a rich and powerful man.

Alice awoke full of happiness that all her concerns would be washed away, if only she could eat the pike. As the sun came up, she woke Maurice and told him of her dream.

'So all we have to do is catch the pike. I'll cook it and we can eat it together.'

Maurice looked at her in the way that men do when they know something is impossible but do not want to disillusion their wives. He tried to explain to her that catching the pike was very difficult, that he had tried many times when he was a lad, and that he knew full well that no one had caught it since. But Alice was having none of it, and so, to keep the peace, he invited her to come to the riverside with him, to find the pike. It took several visits, and Maurice almost believed that she would give up on her quest when: 'Look! See there! That's the pike!'

Indeed it was the pike – and in the excitement of the moment, abandoning any skill that he might have as a fisherman, Maurice clambered down the bank and into the water, trying to catch it with his bare hands. You don't need me to tell you that he didn't catch it. All that happened was that he ended up sitting in the water, midstream, with little tiddlers flapping on his jacket and in his hair.

Well, of course the scene attracted a lot of attention, and Maurice was the cause of much laughter and joking. But the story of the pike and the fortune of the unborn child was now an open secret. Maurice noticed that he suddenly seemed to get more business, as people asked him about his child and whether Alice had 'had her pike'.

The local lads took it upon themselves to catch it. They were sure there would be a reward if they did. But with all the palaver of their rods, nets, sticks and mayhem, none of them were successful. Alice was getting a bit desperate. Her time was coming soon, and no pike was on her table. She could not let her son down.

'If I want a pike', she thought to herself, 'then I am going to have to get it myself.'

Truth be told, that baby was nearly on its way on the day when Alice waddled down to the river. She had in her hand a leather bucket attached to a piece of rope. This was how she was going to catch her fish. She found the place where the carts crossed, and positioned herself so that the bucket floated, with the frayed rope looking like a bounty of worms. She dropped it into the water and waited.

And she didn't have to wait very long. It seemed as if the pike jumped into her bucket within seconds, and she pulled it up. The pike was thrashing around and almost got away, but Alice grabbed it with both her hands. It felt so smooth and delicate. Then she dropped it into her apron, where it continued to thrash against her blooming stomach.

As she made her way to the bank, the local lads applauded her, and she went pink both from embarrassment and exhaustion. The story of her success spread like wildfire through the whole community. That night she and Maurice dined on pike. I'm told it's very tasty with a white sauce. I don't think that Maurice and Alice had that, but I can tell you they both went to bed that night feeling full and very happy.

But it wasn't to last long. In the early hours of the morning the baby started to move and the midwife was sent for. Maurice and Alice were delivered of a fine baby boy, and they called him George. The christening ceremony was the next thing to organise – who should they ask to be godparents?

That was more difficult. Not for the lack of people to ask, but because now there were so many to choose from. The night after the birth came the first of many visitors to their house. These were all gentlemen of the town, who, knowing of her prophecy, and respecting her achievement in catching the pike, came to offer their congratulations on the birth. They mentioned that, by the way, they would be quite happy to support young George in his education as he grew up. All of them were certain that a grateful scholar would remember his sponsors when he was a great man. Maurice and Alice chose three of the men of quality to be his godfathers, and the christening was a day of celebration indeed.

And you know what it's like when you feel you have missed out on an opportunity, and you have a chance to try again? When Alice was pregnant with her next child, certain men of quality visited again, promising to sponsor the child if it was a boy. And it was. And so was the next one. Three boys, and all with promises of sponsorship for their education. Mary was a very satisfied woman. Just having her three sons achieve their education was great enough for her. And those boys didn't disappoint her! George went on to become Archbishop of Canterbury – one of the most influential posts in the land; one brother went on to become Mayor of London; and the other became Bishop of Salisbury.

George always appreciated the place where he was born, and the support he was given. He established Abbot's Hospital in Guildford to help the elderly poor who needed somewhere to live. All her sons achieved more than Alice had ever expected – and it all came about through the promise of catching a really big fish. Sometimes it's good to follow your dreams!

⌒⌒⌒

At the top end of the High Street in Guildford is a statue of George, and at the bottom end, on the other side of the river, is an alehouse that carries George's name. The Abbot's Hospital is on the High Street, and there are sometimes guided tours. On the other side of the street is the Holy Trinity Church, where George has a rather magnificent tomb.

FIVE

THE FAIR MAID OF ASTOLAT

There are many stories of King Arthur and the Knights of the Round Table, but this one takes place near Guildford.

⬤◉⬤

It was midsummer and it was hot. The London court of King Arthur at Westminster was sweltering. In the heat everyone was listless and unmotivated, and petty squabbles frequently broke out. King Arthur knew that he had to do something to focus his Knights of the Round Table, and he had just the idea: a tourney. He would send out messengers with invites for a jousting competition between the knights and the rest of the kingdom. Maybe a few of the comers might be good enough to recruit to his army. It was a great opportunity.

The tourney was set to take place in Camelot. It was much cooler than Westminster as it was closer to the coast, set more in the countryside, in the shade of the trees, and benefited from the breeze of the rolling hills. Nowadays we know it as Winchester, and you can even see the Round Table hanging in the Great Hall. But then it was known as Camelot, spiritual home of King Arthur and the Knights of the Round Table.

There was great excitement and preparations to be made, and everybody was very busy, packing and preparing for the journey. Well, one person wasn't too excited. Guinevere, King Arthur's wife, declined to attend as she said she 'wasn't feeling so well'. Arthur was disappointed.

'This will be the best tourney for the past seven years. You must come. It won't be the same without you there. The people and the knights will be looking for you as my queen.'

It was when Lancelot, Arthur's best knight, also declined to attend that Arthur was really disappointed. 'The people and the knights will be expecting to see you fight. You're a legend and they want to see you!'

But Lancelot had been in too many fights for his king and he was still nursing a few wounds that made his body ache. He could not imagine fighting just for the fun of it. So he said 'No', he'd stay and watch over the Queen. The preparations went ahead for the tourney, and, as the day drew near, King Arthur left with his knights, to establish themselves at Camelot.

The castle in London was very quiet, as almost the whole retinue of servants and knights had gone. Guinevere and Lancelot met in the orchard. When she saw him she blushed, and he found it difficult to breathe. I will tell you a secret. Maybe you already know it. Many years ago they had fallen in love, but she was the Queen, married to the King, and he was his king's best champion. Some say that they expressed their love. Some say that they were honourable to the promises they had made to their king. They lived only for the few minutes and seconds that they were able to share each other's company without being observed and without breaking vows.

I will tell you something else. In battle or tourney, knights would often wear a lady's favour, a scarf or sleeve from the lady, on their armour. There was only one lady for whom Lancelot would carry a favour – and he could not do that openly in case someone guessed of his love for the Queen. If that happened then he, Guinevere and Arthur would all be disgraced, so he never wore anyone's favour. When she saw him in battle, Guinevere's eyes would light up – because she knew that the favourless knight was fighting for her.

Her eyes certainly lit up when she and Lancelot met in that orchard. And in that breathless moment, they both realised that this was reckless. To be together without company could be their undoing. It would be so easy to make a gesture or share a small word of love, thinking that they were alone, but a passing serving boy might see and hear all. Then tongues would wag. Guinevere urged Lancelot to go south, to join the King. Lancelot laughed and told her that he would go and fight, but he would play a trick on the King. He would join the all-comers instead of the King's Company.

Arthur and his company had travelled south and were staying overnight in the village of Astolat. Today it is part of Guildford, but then it was a village with a few houses, an inn or two, and maybe a few fine homes for minor knights and nobility. Arthur was established in the local inn, and, as the sun set, he went for a stroll to clear his head. As he did so, he spotted Lancelot on his horse, turning off the road.

'The old rogue,' thought Arthur, 'He's come after all. I'll wager he will fight in disguise! But he can't fool me.' He chuckled to himself at the thought of thwarting Lancelot's trickery.

When Lancelot was much younger, he had met a knight called Sir Bernard, who had now retired to live outside Astolat. Lancelot planned to ask him for lodging for the night, so that he didn't have to risk meeting Arthur and spoiling his 'surprise'. Sir Bernard was quite old and didn't recognise Sir Lancelot, but was pleased to offer a bed and a fine meal to a Knight of the Round Table.

Some good wine was shared, and a rather jolly Lancelot asked Sir Bernard's help in tricking the King. Sir Lancelot thought that if he used his own shield, he would surely be recognised, so he asked if Sir Bernard had a spare shield that he could use, so that no one would know. Delighted to be included in such a jape, Sir Bernard offered the use of his eldest son's blank white shield. The son was travelling away from home, and the shield was not well known. Into the bargain he offered his youngest son, Sir Lavaine, as a companion to ride with him. All was agreed, with much slapping of backs and laughter at the fun of the deception.

However, Sir Bernard had a third child: Elaine le Blanc. She was much younger than her brothers and her father was very protective of her. She was just old enough to find men interesting, and, when she saw Sir Lancelot, she felt she would faint away at the pleasure of seeing such a beautiful man, so strong, with scarred hands and firm body. It was all she could do to approach him when her father called her in. With her eyes down, she left it until the last moment to look up into his eyes, and in that second all reason was lost to her, and she had to remind herself to breathe. She listened to the talk of shields and disguises in bewilderment. Then boldly she looked Lancelot in the eye, and asked, 'Will you wear my favour?'

For her, it was as close as she would ever come to making a declaration of love. At first Lancelot laughed, and said he wore no lady's favour. That cut through her like a knife. She felt rejected, embarrassed, ashamed. But then Lancelot mused aloud, 'Actually, that would help towards the disguise. No one would suspect me if I am wearing a lady's favour. What do you have to offer me?' Lancelot was being pragmatic, caught up in the game, but those considerations washed over Elaine. All she could think was that he had asked her what favour she had to offer him. She felt like singing, 'Take me, my heart, my maidenhead,' but instead she took her sleeve of red silk with pearls and gave it to him.

'Thank you. That will suffice'. In exchange, he gave her his shield for safe keeping until his return. She held it gently, as though he had given her his heart and soul. Lancelot understood nothing of this expression of love and devotion.

The next morning, Lancelot and Lavaine left for the tourney in Camelot. Sir Bernard and Elaine waved them goodbye. By the time they arrived at Camelot, the noise and bustle was overwhelming. Most of the good billets were gone, and so they lodged at the far end of town. This suited Lancelot very well – less chance of him being recognised. Even Lavaine still did not know who he was.

There were to be three days of the tourney. The Knights of the Round Table would take on all-comers in individual matches, and then there was to be a final melee of all contenders, with the last knight mounted being the overall winner.

Lancelot and Lavaine joined the all-comers' group. As soon as Lancelot began, a murmur went around the field. It was clear that he was swift and experienced, and he soon dismounted many of the King's men who opposed him.

King Arthur was sitting with Sir Gawain, and he gave a wry smile. He knew that this must be Lancelot but he was not going to spoil his fun. Arthur said nothing. Gawain, however, was curious. Who was this knight? Where had he come from? The shield was not one that he knew, yet with such skill he must be a knight of note.

'If I didn't know better,' said Gawain, 'I'd think it must be Lancelot. But he never wears a lady's favour, and that's definitely a red sleeve wrapped around his helmet. So it can't be him.'

The Knight of the Red Sleeve dominated the field, and when it came to the final melee, some of the Knights of the Round Table decided to band together to force him down. Surrounded by the knights, Lancelot fought them off, but not before one of them had accidentally pieced his armour with a spear; the spearhead was broken off in the wound. Despite pain and much blood, Lancelot called Lavaine to his side, and, between them, they routed the rest of the knights. There was no doubt who had won that day.

There was silence and expectancy on the tourney field, and then the Knight of the Red Sleeve was declared the winner. Everyone waited to see the identity of the knight. But no one came forward to claim the prize. King Arthur was disappointed that he would not be able to unmask Lancelot, but declared that the absence of the Knight of the Red Sleeve was the ultimate act of chivalry. It suggested that all the knights who had taken part were winners.

But Lancelot was not being chivalrous. He was in trouble. His old wounds had been aggravated by the fierceness with which he had fought. The final wound from the spear was too much, and he lay seriously wounded. He begged Lavaine to pull the spearhead from his body. As it was withdrawn, he fainted. When he came round, he told Lavaine to take him away, to the house of a nearby hermit, who had a way with healing. But the hermit had spent some time in the world, and recognised Lancelot by the scar on his cheek. Lavaine was stunned to know who his companion was. Lancelot begged the hermit again: 'Help me for God's sake, and for death or life of me put me out of this pain.' The hermit promised to do as much as he could.

At the tourney, the festivities continued with a great feast for the knights and the all-comers. King Arthur sent for the leader of the all-comers and enquired after the Knight of the Red Sleeve. Arthur was shocked to hear that the Knight of the Red Sleeve was badly injured, and he began to fear for his friend. He asked Sir Gawain to search for the Knight of the Red Sleeve, without revealing Lancelot's identity.

Gawain searched six or seven miles all around Camelot, but finally he gave up and started the journey back to London. He decided to lodge with an old friend, Sir Bernard, at Astolat.

Sir Bernard was pleased to see yet another Knight of the Round Table, and asked after the tourney at Winchester. Gawain regaled them with tales of the tournament, and the impact of the two knights with blank white shields, and the one who wore the red sleeve. Elaine could hardly contain her excitement. 'Oh!' she cried. 'That was my favour. That was the man I love so well.'

Gawain was taken aback to have so easily discovered the means to find the identity of the Knight of the Red Sleeve. 'You know this knight? He is your lover? What is his name?'

Elaine was dewy-eyed as she cried, 'Yes and yes!' Then looked downcast as she confessed, 'But I do not know his name. I have the shield he left in place of my brother's.' The whole story was told and the shield was brought out. Gawain gasped when he recognised it.

'Truly this knight has paid you great honour. In all the years that I have known him, never has he worn a lady's favour. Now I am concerned that his shield has stayed here, and Lancelot has not returned to retrieve it.'

He told them of the wounds that the Knight of the Red Sleeve had sustained, and of his disappearance at the end of the tournament. Elaine, thrilled to learn the identity of her knight but distressed at the news of his injuries, promptly declared that she would go in search of her lover and her brother.

Gawain returned to the court of King Arthur and told of everything that had occurred, including the 'great' love that was between Lancelot and the fair maid at Astolat. Guinevere was furious to hear that Lancelot had worn the favour of a lady who also claimed him as her lover, and felt that he had been unfaithful to her. She had to listen, stony-faced, as all the talk at the court was of Lancelot and his 'lover'.

Elaine searched all the places she thought her brother might have taken refuge, and found him just by chance while he was exercising his horse. She was taken to Lancelot's bedside and called him by name. She told him of Gawain's visit and how he had recognised the shield. Lancelot groaned. He knew Gawain would tell the court in London everything, including his wearing of the red sleeve. He was also sure that Guinevere would misinterpret everything.

Elaine stayed to take care of Lancelot, whilst Lavaine went to find Sir Bors, one of the Knights of the Round Table. When Sir Bors arrived back he was shocked to find his friend so ill. He was very surprised at the familiarity with which Elaine cared for Lancelot, and taken aback by Lancelot's blatant disregard for her. Lancelot only wanted news of Guinevere – to know how angry she was. Sir Bors told him all; but in a quiet moment, when they were alone, he had to point out to Lancelot that Elaine was clearly enamoured of him, and warned him to be more discrete. Lancelot brushed aside those concerns.

It was several months before Lancelot felt recovered enough to return to court, and Elaine had cared for him every day. Finally giving thanks to the hermit, Lancelot and Elaine rode back to Sir Bernard's at Astolat. Lancelot's intention was merely to give his thanks to Elaine for her tender care and nothing more. All he could think of was returning to court, to see Guinevere, to make sure she understood that he had not been faithless to her. He still did not realise the depth of the attachment that Elaine held for him, until she called out to him: 'My lord – please do not leave me alone to die of love of you. Let me be your wife. I have tended you so closely during these months, more than a wife would do.'

Lancelot shook his head. 'Thank you for everything you have done but I shall never take a wife. I do know that your care has enabled me to recover and be strong and, as thanks for that, I promise you that when you find a knight to love as well and take as your husband, I will settle on you £1,000 a year.'

He thought that this was a right and generous thing to do. Elaine could not believe her ears. She begged again, and was spurned again. She fainted and was carried away to her room. Sir Bernard was distressed at his daughter's despair, but Lancelot was adamant that he had given her no hope of receiving anything except thanks for her care. Lancelot left for Arthur's court, thinking only of Guinevere. Sir Bernard watched over his youngest child, wondering how long his daughter's sickness would last.

Lancelot was welcomed back to court, with a great slapping of backs and teasing about the Knight of the Red Sleeve. All was known. Guinevere, however, was furious and would not even speak to him. It was all that he feared and worse. He tried to explain, but it did him no good. She would not listen.

Elaine also would not listen. She would not eat, would not sleep; she spent her days and nights weeping, greatly distressed, crying out for her great love Lancelot, and claiming that if she could not have him, she would depart this world. Nothing her father or brother could do would change her mind. Finally she called them both to her.

She asked them to write a letter, which she dictated, and then asked that it be placed in her right hand when she died. She gave instructions for her dead body to be dressed in her finest clothes, laid on a fair bed and taken to the Thames. There, it was to be placed on a black barge and floated down the river until it reached Westminster, where she hoped that Lancelot would see her one last time.

The next day she died, and her father and brother did everything that she asked. As the barge floated down the Thames, Arthur and Guinevere saw it from the castle window and sent their knights to investigate. The messengers told of a fair woman, on a richly decorated bed. Arthur and Guinevere came to see the sight, wanting to know more of this wonder. Guinevere pointed out the note and Arthur took it, hoping to solve the mystery of who she was, and why she was on the barge. Arthur read out the note in court. Malory records it as saying:

Most noble Knight Sir Lancelot.
I was your lover, whom men called the Fair Maid of Astolat:
Therefore unto all ladies I make my moan;
Yet pray for my soul, and bury me.
This is my last request.
Pray for my soul, Sir Lancelot, as thou art peerless.

Lancelot was sent for; the letter was read again and he was asked to give his account. He was shocked to hear of her death, but stood his ground and claimed no responsibility for the depth of her affections. He acknowledged that he was greatly in her debt, but that he could not match the love she had for him. He had given her thanks and offered her a pension. He could not see what more he could have done.

Guinevere pushed him. 'You could have been gentler with her. Found some way to let her down.'

Lancelot stood in front of his queen. He knew that he was speaking to her as his lover, as well as addressing his king and all those present. 'Love arises where it will. It cannot be forced, it cannot be trained. She loved me greatly; I could not love her back. I tried to soften the blow by promising her £1,000 yearly if she set her heart on any other knight. She in turn could not accept this. I can only love where love arises by itself; I cannot love on command.'

Arthur nodded and agreed with the truth of what Lancelot said. There had to be a resolution to the situation, but in all honesty he could think of nothing more than declaring that Lancelot take responsibility for the proper burial of the Fair Maid of Astolat.

So the Fair Maid was buried, and the church services and rites were completed to save her soul. Lancelot tried to understand where he had gone wrong, what he could have done differently. He had been so intent on guarding his emotions for Guinevere that he had been unaware of anyone else's feelings for him. It was a struggle that Lancelot was to continue to face for the rest of his life.

Lancelot and the Queen were eventually reconciled, but what happened next is another story.

⚭

There are many collections of stories about King Arthur, and one of the best is Le Morte d'Arthur *by Thomas Malory, which is where this story comes from.*

SIX

CAPTAIN SALVIN
AND THE FLYING PIG

People often say 'pigs might fly' when they think that something is impossible, but in Surrey we know that nothing is impossible!

⊙⊃⊂⊙

Captain Salvin was a good and experienced soldier. He had fought for Queen Victoria and then retired to his home at Whitmoor Common in Surrey. He was an expert in hawking and fishing and wrote a book so others could enjoy these sports. He loved all kinds of animals, and when two orphaned otter kittens were found, he ordered them to be brought to the house. There he fed and cared for them himself, feeding them milk through the night until they were sure to survive. Nowadays we would probably aim to get them back into the countryside, but in Captain Salvin's day it was very different. Those two otter kittens would curl up on his lap, or climb all over him, sneaking under his collar or inside his waistcoat. They followed him all over the place, and behaved as if they were pet cats. Some people thought it an extraordinary sight to see him walking across the common followed by two otters. Extraordinary? They didn't know what was to come.

Because of his service in the army, Captain Salvin had connections and friends all over the world. The Maharajah Duleep Singh, from India, shared his interest in falconry. He was the last maharajah of the Sikh Empire, and had been exiled to England, where he lived in Norfolk. He came to visit Captain Salvin at Whitmoor Place and brought with him the gift of a Syrian pig. These were very highly regarded, and it would have been an asset to Captain Salvin's breeding stock of pigs. But as soon as the Maharajah left, the pig fell ill.

Captain Salvin wouldn't take the risk of the pig dying, and possibly offending his friend, so once again he ordered a sick animal to be brought to the house. There, again, he fed and cared for it himself, feeding it milk through the night until he was sure it would survive. He called the pig Lady Susan and, just as he had done with the otters, he became very attached to her. He gave her a collar and a small bell, and she became a house pig! She followed Captain Salvin like a dog when he went for walks across the common. When people saw them, they thought it was an extraordinary sight indeed. But they still didn't know what was to come.

As she got bigger, Lady Susan's belly started dragging on the ground, crushing the crops. Captain Salvin tried to think of ways both to prevent her hurting herself, and to stop any complaints about the damage to the crops.

The solution was simple. Just teach her to jump.

Oh, it's simple to teach a pig how to jump. At least, it is if you are Captain Salvin. He didn't know the meaning of impossible. You need a pocket full of apples, and lots of patience. They would go into the woods, and the Captain would jump over a stick on the ground. Lady Susan, of course, would just waddle over. Not quite what he wanted. But slowly and surely Lady Susan learned how to 'jump' over the sticks. Then a log, and then across a stream. It became quite a sight to see them running through the woods and common, leaping over obstacles in their way, and crossing streams without getting wet.

As Lady Susan got bigger and bigger, she started sleeping in a special pig pen built for her. Like all pigs, she had a habit of grovelling in the ground with her snout and creating holes in her pen. Captain Salvin thought he had a solution for stopping this, and an opportunity for a very entertaining trick.

He sent invitations to his friends to come to a dinner, promising them a sight they would never believe. He also invited round a blacksmith to put a ring on Lady Susan's snout – a good way to stop her from digging in the ground with it. The blacksmith was due to arrive at 2 p.m. Captain Salvin wined and dined his friends, then summoned them to the pig sty, where they concealed themselves to await the spectacle.

The blacksmith arrived and was told where the pig was. He thought it was a very stylish pig sty (and may have even mused on how much better it was than his own house!). The sty was fairly large, and Lady Susan had lots of room. When she heard him enter the pen, she got up and came out to see him. Having been treated like a dog, it was her habit to greet people by running up to them and then balancing her front legs on them – just as a dog does. When Lady Susan did this to the blacksmith, he was so surprised that he fell over in the pen. He picked himself up and looked around, only to see Lady Susan coming towards him again – Rum ti tum, Rum ti tum.

He panicked at the sight of this large pig 'charging' him, and looked for a way to escape. But he was trapped – the only way out was over the wall, which was just under 4ft high. He just about scrambled over, falling down the other side. But at least he was safe from the pig. Or so he thought!

The blacksmith sat on the mucky ground, catching his breath. Meanwhile, Lady Susan loved this new game, and, just as the blacksmith had vaulted the wall, so did she – sailing through the air, right over the astonished man.

Captain Salvin and his friends were behind the trees, and saw everything. Now that truly was an extraordinary sight – a pig that could fly! There was much laughter and merriment. The black-smith wasn't happy at being made a fool of, but Captain Salvin gave him a merry fee and all pride was salved indeed. And many a young gentleman dined out on the story of how they saw a pig fly.

So the next time that someone says 'pigs might fly', just remember that, in Surrey, anything can happen!

SEVEN

THE TREACHEROUS MURDER OF A GOOD MAN

What do you do when a good man is brutally murdered? Make examples of the perpetrators! By Hindhead and the Devil's Punch Bowl is Gibbets Hill. There used to be a real gibbet up there. A special one with a circular rail on which the bodies of three men were hanged, tarred and left to rot as a warning to other travellers.

෨෴෪

The date is 24 September 1786. It's a sunny day, but the nights are cold and brutal. In Portsmouth the sailors have long landed, taken their cash, and gone to spend it on wine, women and song. Some have travelled as far as London to savour the fleshpots, eschewing the local establishments in favour of the call of the big town. Many sailors passed their time this way. It's what they all did: blew all their money, and then slowly made their way back to Portsmouth to get the next ship so they could do it all over again.

Very occasionally you got a sailor who had a sensible head on his shoulders, who was careful with his money, making sure that he had a bit to spare to get him back for his next ship. Or maybe he was flush with money because he had taken part in a little roguery himself, cutting the purse of some fine gentleman in London town. Who knows which way the wind blows? But, there was at least one sailor with some cash in his pocket, making his way back to Portsmouth on that fateful September day.

He stopped at the Red Lion Inn in Thursley. A place with a low doorway, where you have to duck or else hit your head on the rail. He thought he recognised a man he had sailed with before. He greeted him, and offered to buy him and his two friends a drink. The three men looked at each other, delighted to find someone so free with his money, and willingly took up his offer.

But do you know, the one he had greeted so warmly just could not place him. He didn't want to affect the other's generosity by admitting to not knowing his name, and so all four shared their own stories of the sea. Ones that could have happened anywhere. They laughed and were generally jovial with each other. And so our man asked if he might join them on the road back to Portsmouth. The presence of brigands and robbers made it sensible to travel in good company, and he had enough to pay for their drinks and food.

This was bliss to the ears of the three sailors, who faced the final thirty miles on foot, and had no prospects of getting food in their bellies other than what they could beg or forage from the side roads. And so it was agreed. Safety in numbers. Well, you would think so, wouldn't you?

We don't know if there was a falling out. We don't know if there was some jealousy. What we do know is that at Hindhead those scoundrels attacked him, killed him, and cut his head from his body. They tore open his haversack and stripped him of his clothes. They laughed as they diced for the spoils amongst them, and then threw the body into the Devil's Punch Bowl. Hoping, perhaps, that the Devil himself would smile upon them and cover their tracks.

But not even the Devil could help them. Unbeknownst to them, they had been seen by two shepherds. With eyes used to scouring the landscape for their sheep, they had clearly seen everything that had happened.

The two shepherds raised the alarm, and the body was found. The men who found it puked their guts out and shook visibly, so shocked were they at the violence inflicted on the body. The shepherds were able to give a fair description of the scoundrels, and knew the direction the robbers had gone.

The three seafarers stopped at the Sun Inn in Rake. They laughed as they toasted each other, and ate a fine meal. Realising that they would need more cash, one of them suggested selling the clothes they had with them, so they could continue their journey in style. One of them sold his entire share of the clothes, and the other two were haggling with the local lads, when the hue and cry arrived in Rake. They were soon spotted by the shepherds, and, after a bit of a scuffle and a fight, the three seafarers were apprehended. The evidence of blood on one of their shirts was enough to confirm suspicion on them.

They were taken back to Hindhead, where one by one they were led into the room where the mangled body lay on the table. Each man kept his mouth shut, as they were in turn made to place a hand on the corpse. It was an old belief that a murdered man's body will bleed if his murderer touches it. And it was a hard man who could look and touch a body without fearing the wrath of the victim. One sailor was more God-fearing than the others; terrified at the thought of being haunted by the dead man, he refused to touch the bloody body. He broke down and confessed everything. The men were taken to the gaol house and from there to Kingston Court.

The *Hampshire Chronicle* of 2 October 1786 records it as a 'shocking murder', and it seems to have touched the hearts of people in the local community – especially when it came out that the three had supped from the generosity of the murdered man.

They were found guilty on Thursday 5 April 1787, and two days later they were taken back to Hindhead, where a gibbet was specially erected to cater for the three. They were hanged, their dead bodies covered in tar, and they swung there for some time as a warning. Local people became too afraid to walk in the area, and after dark they feared that the souls of the scoundrels might come back to haunt them.

Memorial stones were put up both at Hindhead and in the cemetery where the victim was buried, in an attempt to rest his soul. And in all that time, no one could identify the unknown sailor. Careful who you befriend on the road!

∞∞

You can go to the Devil's Punch Bowl today, and take the 'Sailors walk' from the National Trust café, across the re-grassed part of the old A3 (now superseded by the Hindhead underpass), past the place where he was murdered, and on to the Iona Cross – which stands to remind all and sundry of the folly of false friendship, but also to dispel some of the fears and superstitions of local people.

And sometimes, when the wind is whistling through the trees, and whipping up the side of the Devil's Punch Bowl, you may hear the wail of a man betrayed by those he befriended. If you look carefully, you may see his ghost in the illustration.

EIGHT

HOW THE DEVIL'S JUMPS AND THE DEVIL'S PUNCH BOWL CAME TO BE

The Devil seems to have been pretty busy in Surrey, and there are several parts of the landscape named after him. Some of them even have more than one story!

❦

Since the dawn of time, Surrey has faced the conundrum of having belief in both the Christian god and the Norse gods. And for a time they both reigned supreme. But the Devil was always one to stir up a bit of trouble.

Now, Thor kept company with men in Surrey out by a place we call Thursley (Thor's Lee, or just Thor's place). It is a pretty little village, and you can understand why Thor chose to take time out from the world and just chill there. Sometimes he would be working at his anvil, sometimes just resting in the sun, and sometimes sharing good company.

But the Devil, always partial to a bit of leaping and larking about, greatly amused himself by jumping from hill to hill, creating a riot and commotion as he went. We call these hills the Devil's Jumps and they are just outside of Churt.

One day Thor, having a bit of a headache and being irate at the disturbance, started to throw stones and rocks at the Devil to drive him away. One very large rock just missed the Devil, and became imbedded at the top of one of the Devil's Jumps. It was huge, and, once there, it stayed there. No one could move it for a very long time. It became known as Stony Jump – until the hills were bought up, and then the owner levelled the hill to build a house and the rock was gone.

The Devil didn't take kindly to Thor trying to ruin his fun, so he scooped up the earth around him and threw it back at Thor. Thor was just as good at dodging and diving as the Devil, and the Devil kept missing him. Soon enough the Devil had hollowed out a huge dip in the ground, and that's how the Devil's Punch Bowl came into being.

Some people think it's a bit posh that in Surrey, the Devil has a punch bowl. They think that anywhere else in the country it would have been called the Devil's Dip or the Devil's Hole. But I can tell you, all you have to do is go down there in the early morning, or in the evening, when the mists come down and fill the hollow. When you see the mist flowing over the top you will see exactly why it's become the Devil's Punch Bowl.

Other people say that the Devil did indeed make his own punch in this bowl, heating it from the fires in hell, and that the mists are merely the steam rising from the potion he is brewing. But watch out if you try to take a sip. The Devil himself once burned his lips drinking the hot punch from a metal spoon. He was so furious that he carelessly flung away the spoon, which landed in Sussex,

across the border. And I know this to be true because it landed at Torberry Hill, and if you go there today you can see the profile of the spoon and its contents scattered all around.

꿍ꞇꝏ

Some people say there is yet another version of how the Devil's Punch Bowl came to be …

Now, for some reason, the Devil spent a lot of time in both Surrey and Sussex – and his larks weren't confined to one or the other. There was a time, when the Devil was in Sussex, that he became very annoyed at all the churches being built there. Presumably the number of churches in Surrey didn't bother him so much.

The Devil, being the Devil, decided he would try to flood all the churches out of Sussex and keep that land to himself. He planned to dig a channel through the South Downs and then let the waters of the English Channel flow over the land and rid him of all Christendom, in Sussex at least! As he flung the earth aside, it settled to create both the Chanctonbury Ring and Rackham Hill. But the Devil could only work at night when the sun was away. If he hadn't finished his work by the time the sun rose, then he knew he must stop and never complete it. Even the Devil had to stick to the rules!

It was an ambitious plan and the Devil was a bit noisy digging and throwing all the earth around. With that racket he woke up an old woman who lived nearby. At first she thought that maybe it was her aching back keeping her awake. But no – her back was alright, just the odd twinge or two. Maybe it was the cheese she'd eaten before she went to bed that was affecting her. But no – her belly was feeling fine. Maybe it was something outside of the house? And that's when she looked out of the window and could see the Devil and his work. She was horrified. She didn't know exactly what the Devil was up to but, let's face it, anything the Devil is doing is bound to be wrong.

She knew the sun wasn't due up for some time yet, and she feared that the Devil would complete his work. What could she – an old, frail, feeble woman – do to stop the Devil? There wasn't enough time to raise the alarm. If the Devil succeeded, she and hundreds of others would drown in their beds.

Never underestimate a woman, no matter how old, frail and feeble. You don't need brawn to stop the Devil, just a good set of brains and belief in yourself. She found an old metal tray and polished it as hard as she could to make it as shiny as possible. She searched the house, and found her hoard of emergency candles. She placed as many candles as she had in front of the shiny tray, and then lit them. The candles were reflected in the bright metal tray and it was so scintillating that it was as if the sun itself was shining.

The cockerel in her garden was completely fooled and began to crow to welcome the false dawn. One by one all the other cockerels in the area began to wake up, each thinking that he had missed the dawn. Soon all the cockerels were giving their dawn chorus and finally the Devil heard it too.

The Devil was startled. He was sure that he had more time to complete his plan, but he knew the rules. When the sun comes up, he has to stop. Completely. Abandon the project. With a cry of annoyance, he threw one last clod of earth into the sky. But you should never do something in frustration, and he completely missed his aim. It landed far out to sea and became the Isle of Wight. He then turned and leapt back into Surrey, where, let's face it, he felt much more comfortable. But with that grand leap, he landed with such force on the ground that the earth scurried away, and that is really how the Devil's Punch Bowl came to be.

⟨∞⟩

The Devil's Jumps are on private land, and not accessible, but the Devil's Punch Bowl is in the care of the National Trust and is open to those who want to wander the highways and byways. The old A3 is grassed over now, and it makes for an interesting and very pleasant walk. Don't hang around after sunset, though, just in case Thor and the Devil decide to have another fight!

OLD MOTHER LUDLAM AND HER HEALING CAULDRON

Near Old Moor Park, outside of Farnham and Frensham, there is a cave. You can see it from the path, but you can't go in there. It used to be the home of old Mother Ludlam.

༄༅

Now old Mother Ludlam was a wise woman, who lived on the fringes of the villages around Frensham. She was poor and had lost her home. She moved into the caves, and, although it was a bit cold and draughty in winter, in summer it was nice and cool. In the cave, various mosses and lichens grew, and some very rare fungi. Outside there were many wild flowers, weeds and medicinal plants. And what's more, her cave was out of the village.

Because old Mother Ludlam had healing powers, some people may have said that she was a witch. Some people may have said she was just a very wise woman. But most people knew that if you had a pain or a love sickness, then going to see old Mother Ludlam was the best thing to do.

However, asking for a healing potion – be it from a witch or a wise woman – was not the acceptable thing to. But it was perfectly acceptable to ask to borrow something. And so it was, that at midnight, old Mother Ludlam would often find she had a visitor who had come in the moonlight, along the stony path, to borrow a spoon, a ladle, or even a small cauldron. She would smile, and be delighted to lend them whatever they required. Then she would ask: 'Oh – would you like a potion for something while you are here?'

Many a young girl or older woman opened their hearts to old Mother Ludlam, and many a young boy or older man asked for advice. To all of them she gave an ear, whilst stirring away at her cauldron on the fire and then ladling out a potion to take or apply. And within two days, they would return with the borrowed spoon, ladle or even a small cauldron, and perhaps some carrots, parsnips, a loaf, eggs or maybe even a chicken as thanks for the 'loan'. It was a reasonable way to make a living.

One evening, when old Mother Ludlam was stoking the fire and stirring her cauldron, she thought, 'They will be no visitors this night.' The winds were blowing bitterly cold, the rain was pouring down, and there was so much cloud cover that no one would have the moonlight to show them the path. 'Not even the Devil will be out tonight,' she mused.

Suddenly there was a noise at the front of her cave. A footstep on the gravel. She looked up and called out 'Hallo!' By the light of the fire she could just see a shadow at the entrance of the cave. 'Come in, come in. Don't be shy.'

The shadowy figure took a step forward. Old Mother Ludlam turned to greet him. 'Hello,' she smiled, 'what would you like to "borrow"?'

The stranger rasped, 'Your cauldron. I want your cauldron.'

Old Mother Ludlam looked at her shelf where she kept her spare cauldrons. 'Did you want a small one or a large one?' she asked.

'None of those. I want the cauldron you make your healing potions in.'

Now, old Mother Ludlam wasn't sure she liked his tone. And she certainly didn't like the idea of loaning her healing potion cauldron. All her healing arts had gone into that pot. She couldn't let anyone have it. 'I'm sorry. I can't loan you that one, but is there anything else that you want?'

The fire spat and crackled, and a spark flew out close to the stranger. It lit up that part of the cave that was in shadows. Old Mother Ludlam could now see her visitor. His jutting beard, the horns on his forehead, and his impatient pointy tail. It *was* the Devil. Old Nick himself.

She was not going to let him take her cauldron. What would he do with all the healing power in it? Despite standing close to the fire, she shivered. She could feel the perspiration on her upper lip. Her heart felt as though it had been crushed. Her breath was slow. Very slow. Slowly, thoughtfully, loudly, she said, 'No!'

The Devil howled, strode forwards, pushed her aside, and then with his two hands he snatched the cauldron from over the fire. It made no difference to him that human hands would have been scorched black. This was the Devil, and he knew no pain.

Then he went out to the edge of the cave, and in his seven league boots he took one stride and then another and another. And as he put his foot down towards the ground, the earth rose up to meet him. Once, twice, three times. You can see the mounds of earth today – they are known as the Devil's Jumps, just outside of Churt. He took one more large leap to a place we know as Kettlebury Hill. The Devil held the cauldron high and he roared as he laughed.

Old Mother Ludlam was shocked. But not stunned. The Devil was not going to get away with this. No matter what people said about her, she had a broomstick, and she was not afraid to use it! Side-saddle on the broom (after all, she was a lady), she rose up into the air, looking for her cauldron. The winds battered her; it was so wet, cold, bitter and dark. Then it happened.

The wind abated. The rain stopped. The clouds parted. The moon shone.

She could see the Devil about to take another step. She flew down and snatched the cauldron from out of his hands. He was surprised. He was also furious. He stamped his foot again and again at being outwitted by an old woman. He strangled and mangled the ground, until there was a huge hole, and with one final raging foot he disappeared down into hell. And that's how the Devil's Punch Bowl came to be.

And old Mother Ludlam? Flying high, she held her cauldron tight. She knew it was too dangerous to keep the cauldron herself, so she had to find a place to hide it. The best place was the church in Frensham. The people there would keep it safe. She flew down – carefully balancing the cauldron on the handle of her broomstick – until she reached the Church of St Mary the Virgin. She placed the cauldron on the font, gave it one last loving stroke, and made her way back to her cave.

The next day, the people of Frensham were amazed to find the cauldron in their church. Where had it come from? Some people thought it might have been fairies. Some people thought it might have been angels. No one thought it might have been old Mother Ludlam. But it was a big cauldron. Good for brewing ale for the church's wakes days, high days and holy days. Think of all that healing power going into those celebrations.

And old Mother Ludlam? When she got back to her cave, the fire was just about burning, but her cauldron was gone. So what do you do when you lose the mainstay of your life? She picked the largest cauldron off the shelf, dusted herself off, and started all over again.

◌◌◌

You can visit the church at Frensham and see the cauldron. It was originally by the font, but now it's been put close to the altar. Still keeping it safe.

TEN

THE REVENGE OF
WILLIAM COBBETT

William Cobbett was a man renowned for his sense of independence and sense of justice. If he saw anything that he thought was wrong, he was the first to speak up and stand against it.

⌘

William Cobbett was born in Farnham, and his father was both a farmer and a landlord of an inn called the Jolly Farmer. His grandmother lived in Seale in a thatched cottage with two windows. In front of one was a damson tree, and in front of the other was a filbert, or hazelnut, tree. When he visited he would get milk and bread for breakfast, apple pudding for dinner, and bread and cheese for supper. His grandmother made the best smoked herring around, although it was always very smelly when she was 'smoking' it, and on those days William would stay at home.

When William was about eight, he saw the harrier and hounds chasing a hare on Seale Common. They came towards him and he stopped to watch. He was horrified to see the hounds surround the hare, barking and baying, while the huntsmen rode up on their horses. William was angry that the small hare should be so terrified by the hounds, and that it faced imminent death. Despite being

so young, William pushed his way through the hounds and then swiped the hare from the ground into the protection of his jerkin. He could feel the beating of the hare's heart next to his own thundering heart.

The leader of the hounds was a man named Bradley. He was furious with William for interrupting the hunt, and he shouted at William to let the hare go. The hounds were still baying all around him, trying to jump up on him to get into his jerkin, but William would not let go. The huntsman Bradley used his whip to lash out at William, and he caught him across the face. There was now a small trickle of blood on William's face, and the huntsman had no option but to call the hounds away and find another prey.

William waited until they had gone and then released the hare, which ran away as quickly as possible. He wiped the blood off his face then silently watched where the hunt went. He did this for several days. Watching.

William was a lad who took things to heart, and he thought carefully about how to respond. He may have been lashed, but he would find a way to get back at the huntsman and bring him down a peg or two. But he was not one to physically lash back. He would use his brains and think of a way to humiliate the huntsman. He realised that the hunt most often found the hares in one particular area, and that the hares initially ran more or less in one direction. William had a plan!

The next time his grandmother was smoking herrings, he helped himself to a couple and then hid them until the next hunt day. By then the red fish smelt very high! You would have to hold your nose to be in the same room. But William wasn't going to be in the same room. He took the smoked herrings and drew them across Seale Common at a right angle to the usual direction that the hares ran. He knew that the hounds would follow the strongest scent, and the smoked herring was easily a stronger smell than the hares.

He then dragged the red fish on the ground up a steep hill. That would make it very difficult for the horses, and the riders would find it very uncomfortable. Then he went over to the roughest part of the common. He crept through a fence into the heathland and scrubland. The horses wouldn't like that. He did a few swirls around to make sure they went in circles, and then went to the edge of the swamp and threw the remainder of the fish into the middle. He scrubbed himself in stream water to rid himself of the smell, and then he waited.

Sure enough, when the hares were spotted by the hunt they ran in the direction William had predicted. As the hounds came across the trail William had laid for them, he could see their confusion, and hear in their barking that they were unsure. It only took one hound to take up the false trail and the others followed him, with the rest of the hunt after them.

Up the steep hill they went. The horses definitely didn't like that and they slowed down considerably. The huntsmen were lashing their horses to go faster. When they did, they were into the rough common, and more than one hunter came a cropper, falling off as his horse tried to make his path. Bradley was furious when his hounds seemed to go in circles, so when they picked up the scent and were off, he spurred his horse on again. When they reached the swamp, his horse stopped as he felt the ground soften – but Bradley went head over heels and landed in the muddy swamp.

Up in the trees, young William Cobbett was stuffing his fist into his mouth and trying not to laugh too loud. When the huntsmen came by in their black and muddy state, he could hear them blaming Bradley for such a chaotic ride. He was so pleased that his ruse with his grandmother's red herrings had worked.

And that's how we get the expression to 'lay a red herring' – to mislead people about something.

William Cobbett learned two important lessons that day. Firstly, that any kind of bullying or tyrannical behaviour can be challenged, and secondly, that you can use your cunning and wits, not your fists, to overcome it. William went on to travel to France and America, and became well known for always speaking out against injustice, corruption and unfairness. He travelled extensively in England, enjoyed riding, and wrote a diary of all the places he went to, with a note about what was happening on the land and the people he met. It's called Rural Rides *and it's clear that, of all the places he travelled, it was his home county of Surrey that he loved the best.*

You can see the place in Farnham where William was born. It's still a public house, but it's not called the Jolly Farmer any more – it's called the William Cobbett.

ELEVEN

MATHEW TRIGG AND THE PHARISEES

Surrey has its own name for the fairy folk – we call them Pharisees. Nowadays there are only a few pockets of them left, but you still have to watch out that you don't upset them!

❦❦❦

Now Mathew Trigg was a curmudgeonly old man. He and his wife had been together for many years and lived in the village of Ash. They had never had any children, and that was sadness in their lives, but they lived well together. When his wife died, Mathew withdrew into himself. He didn't want to talk to his neighbours, and he most certainly didn't want to talk with the children in the village.

Most of the adults had known him when he'd been the life and soul of the town, so when they saw him walking down the street, they would still call out to pass the time of day. So even if he ignored them, or walked on by, they would feel sorry for him, and regret that he wasn't able to enjoy life any more.

But the children, well, they only knew him as a cantankerous old man. He'd walk through the village every day, dragging his foot and leaning on his blackthorn walking stick. One would run up to him and call out, 'Tell us a story', and he'd wave them away with that walking stick. Sometimes the children would dare each other to touch the edge of his coat, and then turn and run like the clappers before he saw them. You lost if he spotted you! Sometimes they would stand in the shade of the woods, and one would pick up a stick and pretend to be Mathew shuffling by, to choruses of laughter from the other children. Their parents would tell them to hush, and not be so mean to the old man – he'd had a hard time, they said. But children are children …

And it was the children who noticed when Mathew went missing. He always went walking in the early evening, in the twilight. The time between day and night; the time when two worlds pass together and touch briefly. The children hung around in the usual places, but they didn't see him go by. When they asked, no one seemed to have seen him since the previous day. One of the children told their parents, and, being concerned for the old man, they went to check his house. There was no one there, but on the table were the remains of a meal from the previous day. It seemed that he must have gone out at his usual time and not come back.

'Halloo! Halloo! Mathew – where are you?'

Mathew was nowhere to be found in the village. The call went out to help look for him. All the villagers came. The ones with small children left them with the wise old woman at the edge of the village. Holding torches high in the evening sun, they scoured the route that Mathew usually took. The children were asked where they had last seen him. What had they done to him? Had they upset him?

'No,' said Johnny, 'I just asked him for a story. I didn't try to trick him.'

But the children were quite scared. Was it something they had done? Had they taken the teasing too far? They came to the wood, where it was getting quite dark.

'We'll go in as a line,' said one of the adults. 'Everyone, man, woman and child, hold hands, and then stay together as we walk through.'

Someone asked if the children should be there. An unspoken fear about what they might find was at the back of their minds. But another voice said that with the children there they could cover more ground, and time was a necessity now that it was getting darker. If Mathew was in the woods, he must have been there for a day already; they couldn't leave him for another night.

'Halloo! Halloo! Mathew – where are you? Can you hear us?'

Every now and then they would all stop and listen. It would take a while for everyone in the line to get the message, so there was a bit of swaying and moving about. That was just when Johnny spotted Mathew's blackthorn walking stick lying on the ground. He called out, and everyone came to see. And the adults gasped! The children were confused. What was the matter? One of the mothers pointed.

'Can you see the ring of toadstools? He must have stumbled into a fairy ring. The Pharisees have taken him. The Pharisees have taken him.'

One woman sobbed, and clung to her husband. The other men shook their heads, and the mothers gathered their children to them. 'Out of the woods, come out of the woods. Step carefully, do not step on the fairy rings, else the Pharisees will take you.'

Johnny asked, 'What's happened to Mathew?'

His mother sighed. 'He must have walked into the fairy ring. I guess that with his dragging foot he probably knocked over some of the toadstools. Being in the ring was bad enough, but breaking it! They've taken him away and there's nothing that we can do to get him back.'

Johnny was horrified. He looked back at the trampled ring of toadstools and saw that the blackthorn stick was still lying there. He ran back to pick it up.

'Johnny!' his mother called. He saw the fear in her eyes.

'It's alright,' he said, 'I've just picked up the stick. '

When each child was put to bed that night, there was fear and trepidation written on the faces of their parents. If the Pharisees were back, great care would have to be taken when going into the woods. Daylight only; no liminal visits at twilight or the dark evening. In the morning, the children gathered together, still shocked by the previous day. Johnny had brought the walking stick and they took turns holding it and looking at it. Hoping, perhaps, that it would give them some answers.

'Was it our fault?' one said.

'No,' came a voice. The wise old woman was standing by them. 'Not your fault. It comes from a man who goes into the woods to speak to his dead wife in the twilight. They used to do that when she was alive. They would walk the woods together, and sit on the mound to watch the sun go down. He goes there when he is especially lonely to talk to her. It is just unfortunate that the Pharisees have also taken up residence on his pathway.'

Where had he gone?

'Ah, the Pharisees have an interesting network of places that they live. Come with me, and we shall see what we shall see.'

The children crowded into the house of the wise old woman. Most of them had been cared for by her at some time in their lives, so they knew it well. In the middle of the room was a wide bowl. No one had any idea what it was made of. Some thought crystal, some thought dragon's rock, but whatever it was, they knew that when she poured water in it, pictures came into their minds.

'Let's have a look. Think about Mathew. Think about him now. Where he might be. What he might be doing.' Each child thought hard. Some closed their eyes, and some looked at the floor and ceiling, or even their shoes.

'Ah yes, look into the bowl. Can you see?'

At first it was blurry, but slowly each child managed to work out a picture of Mathew. He was surrounded by Pharisees, who were jeering at him. And Mathew was dancing. Dancing? Yes, dancing!

'Oh,' said Johnny. 'He's at a party. He's dancing. So he is alright!'

The wise old woman looked at Johnny. 'Look again. Look at Mathew's face.'

They all looked again and gasped. Mathew had a look of great pain on his face. It was screwed up, and every time his dragging foot hit the ground his face would twist more with pain. And they could see that he was breathing badly, in fits and starts.

'Oh no,' said the wise old woman. 'Those Pharisees are really punishing him hard. As he broke their dancing circle, they are making him dance and dance and dance. They will make him dance until he dies.'

One of the small girls gave a wail, and turned her head into her sister's arm.

'What can we do?' asked Johnny. 'There must be something we can do.'

'Well,' said the wise old woman, 'there is a potion I could make that would help, but I would need something from each of you to go into it.'

They asked what she needed.

'Something that is important to you, that you would be willing to give up to help Mathew. It has to be yours, mind, not someone else's.'

The small girl turned. 'Something like my dolly?'

'Yes,' said the wise old woman, 'if it's important to you, then that's what is needed. And you must be prepared to give it up.'

'My teddy?'

'My knife?'

'My book?'

'Yes, yes – and what would you give up?'

The children ran as fast as they could to fetch their important things to give up for Mathew. They had seen the pain on his face, and it was as if they had wings on their feet.

When all the important things were placed in her bowl, the wise old woman clicked her fingers. In a moment everything was aflame, and then turned to ash. A look of horror came over the children's faces when they realised that their important things had

really gone. But the wise old woman had no thought about that. She meant business. She took out some oil, herbs and spices and mixed them into the ash. Then she muttered a few words under her breath.

'Now, can someone ask Farmer Giles for use of his horse Dobbin? And tell him not to worry; he will get Dobbin back safe and sound.'

Dobbin was an old farm horse. He had already been put out to pasture, and his long days of service were over. He was a little puzzled to be taken from his field, and led along the path to the wise old woman's house. Surely they were not putting him back into the field with the plough at his back. But he recognised the wise old woman, and whinnied as he thought of the many apples she had slipped him.

'Good Dobbin, now, good Dobbin.' She brought her hands up to his ears and scratched them. Dobbin neighed with pleasure.

'Now Dobbin, I want you to find Mathew Trigg. He is at the other end of the county. Bring him straight back to me. Straight back, mind!' She muttered a few more words, and then rubbed the potion of important things on his back.

A lump appeared; then it grew and stretched and turned into a pair of splendid wings. As Dobbin stretched them out, he whinnied and neighed with the sheer joy, remembering his youth and how he could race the field and jump the hedgerows.

'Remember, straight back to me.'

Then up, up into the air he went, hovering over the village of Ash, where every man, woman and child looked up, wishing him well. And he was gone.

Mathew, meanwhile, was having a very hard time. He could not remember a single second of his life when he wasn't dancing. His foot ached, his belly was empty, his breath racked hard through his lungs as the Pharisees danced around him in turn, taunting him, provoking him, but never letting go of their power to make him dance.

'I shall die here,' he thought. 'Alone and far from home, with no one to care about me, and only these Pharisees torturing me.'

He tried to say again and again how sorry he was to have disturbed them, but the Pharisees had only one thought in mind: vengeance! Mathew began to lose hope. He looked up to the sky as his feet spun, capered and rocked beneath him.

What was that in the sky? Was that a horse? A flying horse? His mind must be going. It was a horse, and what's more it was Dobbin. He'd known Dobbin as a foal; watched as Farmer Giles had put him to the plough; stopped by the fence with his wife and smuggled an apple or two to him when no one was looking.

It truly was Dobbin. As Dobbin hovered above the ground, Mathew capered up, and to the astonishment of the fairies (and himself) he caught hold of Dobbin's mane, and scrambled onto his back. The Pharisees shook their tiny hands most fiercely, but Dobbin was unperturbed and having a whale of a time! High up into the air they travelled, and Mathew was most astonished to see the landscape of Surrey beneath him. Soon he could see the church at Ash, and he knew he would be home before long.

Except for one thing. You remember when the wise old woman said, 'bring him straight back to me?' Well, if you drew a straight line between the place where the Pharisees were, and where the wise old woman was, it would go straight through the church spire in the village of Ash.

All the villagers were looking in the sky for Mathew and Dobbin's return. And suddenly they realised that Dobbin was going to hit the church spire. They called out to turn right, or to turn left. But Dobbin couldn't hear them.

Crack! Dobbin hit the tower. Mathew slid off and found himself clinging to the parapet around the spire and Dobbin floated safely down, where his wings disappeared as soon as he reached the ground. Ladders were brought, and two men climbed the tower to bring Mathew down. The spire was well and truly bent.

And Mathew? Well, they got him down safely – he was just utterly exhausted, and overwhelmed by all the care and attention given to him by the villagers.

In the evening, the wise old woman came to see him, with Johnny carrying his walking stick. But Mathew didn't need the walking stick any more – he'd danced the pain away. But now, when he walks through the village, if the children call out 'Tell us a story', he stops and tells them how their parents and grandparents helped to get him back from the Pharisees. He still goes to talk to his wife, but now he's not so lonely or so curmudgeonly!

And that church tower was bent for a very long time, until the middle of the nineteenth century when a benefactor paid to have it repaired. If you go there now, it's as straight as a die. In the meantime, when you go for a walk in the woods, watch out for the toadstool rings, in case the Pharisees are about!

TWELVE

THE SURREY PUMA

The Surrey puma is a myth that has really captured the imagination. There are many reports of a very large cat, seen in the distance, somewhere in the green fields of Surrey. The Fortean Times *of February 2003 reported that in a two-year period, 362 reports of the Surrey puma were made in Godalming alone. It's not unusual to see an overly large cat in the distance and wonder if it is the Surrey puma. I've done it myself. Surrey also boasts some of the fattest pigeons and squirrels! Why not an over-large tom cat?*

The stories are ingrained in the history of Surrey. In 1770, William Cobbett recorded that in Waverley Abbey there was a hollow elm tree:

> *… into which I, when a little boy, once saw a cat go, that was as big as a middle sized spaniel dog … when in New Brunswick I saw the great wild grey cat, which is there called a lucifee and it seemed to be just such a cat as I had seen at Waverley.*

So what is it that people have been seeing and reporting for the best part of 250 years? For the past few years I have been telling stories in local schools, and I suppose I have become responsible for introducing tales that 'explain' local phenomena, which in turn have entered the local canon of folk tales. One story I tell introduces the Surrey puma, and is based on an old Chinese myth.

Back in the mists of time, when the world was first created, the gods decided that they would choose one animal above all the others to look after the earth, to ensure that everything ran smoothly and to keep an eye on all the other animals. The animal they chose was the cat. They gave the cats the power of speech, to enable them to communicate with all the animals.

For a long time this worked well, and cats were well respected and revered for their thoughtfulness and wisdom. In many cultures they were raised almost to the level of gods themselves. But, you've seen cats, haven't you. The way they like to lie and stretch and curl up, just to feel the sun on their backs. Perhaps they liked that too much. When the creator gods came to see how the cats were getting on with the world, the cats were just resting in the sun. The creator gods asked: 'How are you managing the smooth running of the world?'

'Miaow.' The cats confessed that they mainly let it run by itself, so that they could enjoy the simple pleasures of life. The creator gods were not too happy, and asked the cats to take a more active role in maintaining the smooth running of the world.

'Miaow,' the cats said, 'we'll try.' But when the creator gods came again, the cats were still stretched out in the sunshine, batting at the butterflies that came close to them. Again they were asked how they were managing the smooth running of the world.

'Miaow.' The cats confessed that sometimes it was boring, and they much preferred to enjoy the sunshine. The creator gods were still not too happy, and asked the cats to take an even more active role in maintaining the smooth running of the world. They were, after all, the creator gods' chosen favourite.

'Miaow,' the cats said, 'we'll try.'

But alas, alack. A cat is a cat, and when the creator gods came down a third time, again the cats were enjoying themselves – chasing after dandelion fluff, jumping up to catch it as it floated between the trees.

This time the cats didn't even wait for the question. 'Miaow,' they said. 'We've had enough. It's really too much work for us; we don't want the bother of running this world. There's another creature that likes getting things organised and sorted out. The humans. They are funny little creatures, always busy, busy, busy. Never enough time to enjoy themselves. Why don't you ask them, and we can get back to the business of enjoying all of life's pleasures.'

The creator gods shook their heads. They were disappointed that their favourites had let them down. So they agreed to appoint the humans to look after the day-to-day business of the world. With the job and responsibility went the power of speech and communication. The humans seized the role with both hands, and started to shape the world into the way they wanted it to be. The cats were left with no voice other than their purring.

But the creator gods had already given the responsibility of maintaining the life engine of the world to the cats, and they couldn't take that away. Their purring is the sound of the motors moving the world around the stars, and, should the cats stop purring, then the world will stand still in the sky, and the seasons and all time will come to an end. That's why it's so important that the cats continue to enjoy all of life's little pleasures, even if they no longer look after the world.

And sometimes, those big cats still come to earth to enjoy the sweetness of the countryside, to stroll along the highways and byways of their favourite places. And the beauty of the Surrey landscape still calls out to at least one big cat, so that it returns again and again, just to check what the humans are doing. If he thinks they are doing fine, then he slips away unseen. If not, then he leaves a glimpse of himself to remind the humans that they too can be replaced as the world's guardians, if they are not up to the job!

So watch out! If you see the Surrey puma, maybe it's because you are not looking after the landscape as well as you could be.

THIRTEEN

NOT SO
WISE MEN

THE HERMIT OF PAINSHILL

The pleasure gardens of the eighteenth century were many and various, particularly in London and out in the suburbs. They were a way of being creative with the landscape, producing different effects and evoking emotions in the public who paid to enter them.

⁂

Charles Hamilton had a vision. He had taken two grand tours of Europe and was greatly influenced by what he had seen of the art, architecture and landscapes of Italy. Now he wanted to create a landscape that would thrill and entertain his friends and acquaintances, but also give them cause to think and meditate on the world. He wanted to bring the passion and beauty of classic paintings into the landscape, so that he and his friends could step into them and experience them in all dimensions, and changes of mood. Most importantly, he wanted to include a section that provoked a mood of solemnity and deep reflection. A place to reflect not only on the glory of the landscape, but also on the importance of the Christian god in their lives.

He had bought land in Painshill, Cobham, and over the years he built a ruined abbey, a Gothic tower, and a Turkish tent. Each of them, he felt, could stand alone as a place to explore and to wonder at. The buildings did not need anyone to explain them, or people to populate them. They conveyed their own story.

But something was troubling him. There was one building that he felt needed more to it. He had built a hermitage as part of the gardens; somewhere he could escape to and reflect on his life and the glory of what he had achieved. He realised that the mood he wanted to create was a slight tension between the openness of the other buildings and the reverence of solitude. He felt that he could best achieve this by employing a hermit to live in the hermitage. Visitors would be able to observe him, and yet not approach him. Maybe they would even be afraid of the wild man in the woods.

But not everyone wants to be a hermit, living in seclusion and private contemplation, and anyway, where was he going to find one? He would advertise!

> Wanted
> One Hermit
> To live for seven years in a cave provided
> at Mr Hamilton's Garden, PainsHill, near Cobham in Surrey
> To live a life of contemplation and separation.
> Not to speak to anyone (except Mr. Hamilton).
> Not to shave, nor cut toenails or hair
> All necessities of life provided
> Payment of £700 at the end of the seven years.

There was one applicant, and Hamilton presented him with:

> … a bible, optical glasses, a mat for his bed, and a hassock for his pillow, an hour glass for his time piece, water for his beverage from the stream that runs at the back of his cot, and food from

the house which was to be brought to him daily by a servant, but with whom he was never to exchange one syllable: he was to wear a camblet robe, never to cut his beard or his nails, to tread on sandals, never to stray in the open parts of the grounds, nor beyond their limits.

Hamilton's vision was now complete. He could invite his friends, and create a frisson of fear when they came across the 'unruly wild man'!

However, things didn't turn out as he planned. While Hamilton was able to transform the landscape into a completely different form, he was soon to learn that it was different with a real person. Trees and bushes can be trained, lakes can be dug and sculptured, buildings can be fashioned and aged, but real people will always have their own way, even with the temptation of £700 after seven years. Alas for Hamilton, the hermit was dismissed after three weeks, after he was found drunk in the local tavern!

⬤

Hamilton took heed from this lesson, and didn't try to populate his gardens with people again. Nonetheless, they were the talk of London town, and, even today, the restored gardens are a delight to walk through.

COCKER NASH

It had been a good night for Cocker Nash. He was a fish hawker, and travelled from town to town with his donkey loaded with fish. He had had a surprisingly good day at the markets and the big houses, and there was plenty of cash jingling in his pocket. So he allowed himself a treat. Just a small drink.

The young men in the tavern encouraged him to tell the tales of his younger days, all the time making faces behind his back.

You know the kind of tricks that young men get up to. But Cocker Nash didn't mind. He enjoyed regaling them with tales of his time in the army. As long as someone kept replenishing his pint pot, he had a tale to tell. You could almost believe that he had won the war all on his own. He had led an assault, he said, across the water in Spain – running across the plain while there were shots all around him. And he told of the time he had rescued the lovely Spanish maiden from the burning tower. And the moment when the general had called Cocker Nash to his tent, and told him he was the bravest man in his unit. Those were the days. Cocker Nash shook his head. 'Nothing,' he said, 'nothing can scare old Cocker Nash!'

Maybe he had a drink or two more than he should. Maybe he shouldn't have tried to find his way home in the dark, when there was no moon. Maybe he was blind drunk. But whatever the case was or wasn't, he got lost in the woods of Waverley.

So much for the brave soldier lad. It can be very dark and frightening in the woods. A rustle here, a snap of a twig there, the swoosh of an owl as it flies on its way. The scurry of creatures in the undergrowth. And no light to show the way home. It was too easy to fall into a ditch, and end up sleeping there for the night.

Using all his skill and cunning of the old army days, Cocker Nash knew what to do. 'Man lost!' called out Cocker. 'Man lost!'

He listened carefully, in case someone heard him, but there was no answer. It was getting colder, the mists were creeping in, and he could barely see in front of himself. He had no idea where he was. He tried again. 'Man lost!' he cried. 'Man lost!'

No reply. Cocker was beginning to despair. It seemed that he was going to have to spend the night under the trees. Then he heard, 'Who? Who?'

Huzzah! Someone had heard him, and was asking for his name! 'It's me!' he cried. 'It's me, Cocker Nash from Farnham!'

He heard again, 'Who? Who?'

And again he replied, 'It's me, Cocker Nash from Farnham!'

A third time he heard, 'Who? Who?'

Now Cocker was getting desperate, and in his loudest voice he called back, 'Cocker Nash from Farnham!' He thought he had been found. But it was merely the pigeons calling out, 'Coo, Coo. Coo, Coo.' And Cocker Nash sank to his knees. It was to be a night under the trees for him. But surely this tale was worth a pint in the pub when he got back there!

FOURTEEN

THE GOLDEN FARMER

'Stand and deliver!' The three words travellers do not want to hear. But if you were travelling out of London on the Great West Road down to Salisbury or Exeter in the seventeenth century, you were likely to come across a highwayman or two — especially if you were wealthy enough to afford travel in a coach.

Bagshot Heath was one of the worst places. It's called Camberley now, and it's a very nice place to live; but in those days, if you were travelling through it, you were always advised to carry two purses. A small one to give up freely to the highwayman, and a large one, concealed about your person, to keep for yourself.

There were several public houses in Bagshot Heath, set up to give travellers overnight accommodation and a change of horses, and William Davies often drank in one of them. He was a very well-known farmer in the area and had eighteen children. He'd married an innkeeper's daughter, and knew all the ways of the inns. He also had a small business in London town, selling corn. All in all he was a successful man and well respected. People called him the Golden Farmer because he always paid his bills in gold coins. No paper money, just gold coins.

He would sit with his companions in the inns and listen to the stories of the knights of the road. The people who had been robbed would peer out of the spy holes in the shutters to keep an eye out for highwaymen. And William would watch the travellers who were setting out on their journey west, and listen to their whispered conversations as they worried about their precious belongings, and where they should hide them from the gentlemen of the road. And he would smile.

William Davies was no ordinary farmer. No country simpleton. He led a double life. He was the very same highwayman that plagued the Great West Road.

He was just a lad of twenty-two when he first played at being a highwayman, and found it surprisingly easy. It helped that he was always very polite and had charming manners, so that his victims always felt relatively at ease and safe when handing over their valuables. He soon learned that gold coins were the safest to take. Jewels and watches were difficult to sell on, too easily identifiable, and he always faced the risk of the fence turning him in. Wherever possible he only took gold coins. Nobody ever cottoned on that the highwayman who only took gold was the same local farmer who only paid in gold!

His patch extended from Bagshot Heath to Salisbury Plain, and he became a master of disguise. Sometimes he dressed as a parson, a gentleman or even a banker. Once he robbed the Duchess of Albemarle close to Salisbury Plain. She had a postilion (a driver) as well as a coachman and two footmen. Despite the overwhelming odds, he beat them all to the ground, and then demanded his price from the lady. No gold coins here – so to make it worth his while he took three diamond rings and a gold watch. He even gave the wretched woman a sermon on the sins of painting her face, and the retribution she would get at judgement day, as well as a telling off for being so stingy in her treatment of her servants.

William also robbed close to home and took great risks of being recognised. One day his landlord called to collect the year's annual rent. Quite a tidy sum. William paid up, all in gold coin of course, and then waved the landlord goodbye. Then out the back, after

a change of jacket and hat, he whipped his horse across country to cut off the landlord on the road, appearing to come from the opposite direction.

'Stand and deliver.' The landlord's blood ran cold, and he knew he had no choice but to hand over the money, feeling very foolish that he was carrying so much gold. If only he had asked Davies to pay the annual rent in the town, or came with a guard. Too late.

Did it not strike him that there might be something familiar about the highwayman? The tone of voice perhaps, or the way he tilted his head? Fear was enough to drive all sensible thought from his head. He returned to the inn to find Davies already seated there. In the company of similarly morose men, he recounted how he had been relieved of the gold and was most touched when Davies bought him a drink.

Davies wasn't the only highwayman operating on the Great West Road but he was certainly the smartest. He soon found out if other highwaymen were operating in the area and either gave them due warning to clear off, or invited them to collaborate and share booty. Thomas Sympson was one comrade, and he became known as 'Old Mob'.

Another was Captain O'Brian, who robbed Nell Gwyn on Bagshot Heath itself. He was so charming that Nell, never being slow in coming forward, gave him a kiss. He in turn was so touched that he gave her the jewellery back. In turn again, she gave him 10 guineas for his trouble. King Charles never got a better deal!

In all the years William Davies led his double life, his wife and family never suspected and he never got caught. He gained enough so that he could buy his own farm from the landlord. Eventually he retired from life as a highwayman, and enjoyed the pleasures of the farm, his business, and his grandchildren.

Except that life never turns out quite as you expect. Davies had a chance to expand his farm by purchasing the adjacent land, thus increasing the inheritance for his children and grandchildren. Unfortunately, he didn't have enough ready cash to complete the deal. So he fell back on the only sure-fire way to make money: being a highwayman.

But we all know what it's like when you haven't been very active in an occupation for a while. Your muscles aren't so finely tuned, you forget small details, and you become careless. William had forgotten how well his farm and his business in London were doing, and how well known he had become. He held up a series of coaches outside of London, and on the last occasion the passengers fought back. Being a highwayman was now a young man's game; not a suitable occupation for a man of sixty-four. When the bullet creased into his shoulder, he fell from his horse and his face was unmasked. He was instantly recognised, and he fled from the scene.

He went into London, where he felt no one would know him, and sought sanctuary in Salisbury Court, which he thought would be a safe place. It was a place where debtors went to gain respite from their debt collectors. But he was disturbed, tried to escape and was chased by a butcher. Desperate to get away and hampered by his wound, Davies turned and fired on his pursuer. The man fell dead. Not so nimble on his feet, Davies was overcome by several other men, and brought to the ground.

He was taken to court at Newgate. There was uproar in the courtroom as all the pieces of the puzzle were brought together. William Davies was charged with the murder of the butcher, and then messages came from Bagshot claiming that the man held in Newgate was the same man who was being sought for highway robbery. The lawmakers danced with jubilation when it was revealed that they now had the man who was responsible for forty years of highway robbery, and was the leader of one of the most efficient gangs.

His wife and family were shocked, but their pleas for leniency were not heard and they were not allowed to visit Davies in prison. Simple hanging was too kind for highwaymen! He was hanged at Salisbury Court, the scene of the murder, as a warning to those who took shelter there and tried to abuse the notion of sanctuary. Then his body was cut down and taken to Bagshot, where he had committed his crime. The corpse was tied up in a tarred canvas bag, and left to rot from a gibbet for all to see. Every man, woman and child who travelled out of London on the Great West Road would pass the rotting body of William Davies, golden farmer and highwayman extraordinaire.

His family were devastated, and their business soon went to ruin. There were rumours that Davies had golden treasure stashed away, but nobody ever found it.

⊙◑⊚

An inn near where he lived was renamed the Golden Farmer, which in turn became the Jolly Farmer. Now it's a retail business. But not far away you can find Gibbet Lane, where they hung up the rotten corpse as a warning. If you stand in the lane at dusk, and close your eyes, you can just hear the sound of a canvas bag creaking and a rope stretching in the wind.

FIFTEEN

THE CURFEW BELL SHALL NOT RING TONIGHT

There was a dark time in England's history when a man could support his king, yet find himself a fugitive, accused of treason. A time when a woman could love a man so much, that she would face pain and injury to save him.

It was May 1471 and Blanche Heriot danced at the May celebrations in Chertsey, looking forward to the day that her lover, Neville Audley, would return to her and they could be wed. It was the time of the Wars of the Roses, and he supported the House of Lancaster and the right for Henry VI to be on the throne.

As the May Day celebrations came to an end, so did the world as Blanche knew it. Word had come that there had been a great battle at Barnet, with the Houses of Lancaster and York against each other. And the House of York had won, with Edward IV declared king. Neville was now a hunted man.

After dark there was a scratching at Blanche's front door, and her father woke her with the news that Neville had arrived. She found him in a dirty and dishevelled state. The battle had gone badly wrong, and, in fleeing for his life, cleanliness had taken second place to hiding from the Yorkist soldiers.

He had come, he said, to bid her farewell. He was fleeing to the Continent, where the supporters of Henry VI would reconsider their future. He did not dare stay in England. There was a price on his head, and even now he was hunted. He did not know when he would be able to see her again, but he declared his undying love for her.

He gave her a ring, and swore that he would return to be her husband. He told her that the ring had belonged to one of the Yorkist nobles, for whom Neville had done a great service in the past, and if anything should happen to him, she was to use it to her best advantage. She pleaded with him to stay the night, but he did not want to put her and her family in danger. He would go to Chertsey Abbey and claim sanctuary there until he could move on. He held her tight, stroked her hair, and left.

Blanche could not sleep that night, and in the morning she begged her father to allow her to go to Chertsey Abbey to see Neville. He agreed, but asked her to travel with his friend Herrick, to keep her safe on the road. She agreed – she would do whatever it took to see Neville. The thought of him leaving the country was distressing and she knew she must see him again.

As they travelled to the abbey, they met some Yorkist soldiers who demanded to know their business. There had been an incident the previous night, and one of their soldiers and a dog had been killed. Confronted by the soldiers, Blanche found it difficult to breathe, but Herrick dealt with them smartly and they went on their way.

As they approached the abbey, they could hear noises – horses, and men shouting. The gates of the abbey were open; Neville had been overcome and marched out of the abbey's sanctuary. The soldiers pushed back the onlookers, but Blanche called out, 'Neville!' He looked around and caught her eye. She caught her breath as she saw his bruised and beaten face. He gave the slightest shake of his head, and then looked away.

Herrick found out where they were taking him, and they travelled there. It was not long before there was an announcement that the Lancastrian traitor Neville Audley had been found guilty of treason and would be hanged when the curfew bell rang the next day.

Blanche almost fainted as she heard this. But she also knew what she must do. She turned to Herrick and gave him the ring that Neville had given her. She told him the story. 'Go to London,' she said. 'Find this Yorkist noble. Tell him that Neville's life hangs in the balance, and that he must act to repay his debt.'

Herrick left to ride to London. He was not sure what kind of reception he would get, or even if he would be able to find this Yorkist noble, but he would try. He had seen the look on Blanche's face, and remembered the power and strength of young love. He would do his damnedest to help her and Neville.

There was little else Blanche could do but stand and wait, hoping for a glance of Neville but dreading seeing what injury had been done to him. By evening her father had come to find her. Word of the arrest had reached him, and he had guessed where she might be. He persuaded her to come home that night, and promised he would return with her at dawn.

The night was a sleepless one for Blanche, and, up with the sun, she travelled back with her father. All day she kept watch, but there was no sight of Herrick. There was some building work being done in front of the courthouse, and Blanche felt her stomach tighten as she realised that this was the gibbet on which Neville was to be hanged. She found herself shaking as she watched it develop.

Where was Herrick? He must be coming back soon! Her father reassured her; if it could be done, then Herrick would do it.

As the chorus of birds heralded the fading sun, Blanche was gripped with fear. She must see; she must know where Herrick was. The highest place around was the abbey curfew bell tower itself. She slipped away from her father and made her way there. The door was unlocked and she slid in. The steps up were unsteady, and it was dark and dusty. But she finally stood at the window by the top of the tower. The bell hung next to her, silent but for the creaking of the rafters and the rising chorus of the birds' evening song. She looked out, towards the direction she hoped Herrick would take.

There, in the distance, was a rider. A rider beating his horse to make it run faster. Herrick. It must be Herrick. At first she was filled with joy, but then she had the chilling realisation that from that direction Herrick would have to take the Laleham ferry. A shorter route, yes, but only if the ferry was in the right place …

Oh no! From her vantage point she could see that the ferry had just left the further shore. Herrick would have to wait until it returned.

The evening chorus swelled, and would soon peak. She could hear the sexton's boot on the stairway as he came up to the landing where the bell ropes hung.

Blanche looked at the horizon, then at the gibbet. Neville had been brought out, and already had a noose around his neck. She could see him scouring the crowd – hoping to see her, but wishing she was not there to see him die. She wanted to call out to him, to let him know that he would not die alone. Then a thought came to her. When the curfew bell rang, if he died, she would throw herself from the tower and they would be reunited in death.

When the curfew bell rang? Of course! The sentence had said that he would die at the curfew bell. If it did not ring, then Neville could live.

Below her she could hear the sexton taking up the bell rope. No time to think about it. She crouched down on the boards and ducked under the bell. Bracing herself, she reached out for the clapper. And held on. Tight.

The sexton was puzzled. He was surely sounding the bell, but no ringing came from it. There was no noise apart from a thud and maybe a gasp. Two of the Yorkist soldiers entered the bell tower, and demanded to know the reason for the delay.

It was sunset. The bell must ring. The traitor must die.

The sexton shook his head. He would investigate. He climbed the stairs to the bell tower, and was astonished to find a young woman there, grasping the bell clapper as if her life depended on it. Bloodied, bruised and barely conscious.

He called to the soldiers to help him get her down. As he was doing that, they heard shouts from down below. Herrick rode into town, calling out, 'A reprieve! A reprieve! Neville Audley shall live!'

And with that cry, Blanche let go of the clapper and lost consciousness. The noose was taken from around Neville's neck. The gibbet was taken down. Herrick was well rewarded.

And there was a wedding. Such a wedding you have never seen! Herrick was the guest of honour. Both the bride and groom were covered in bruises, and black-eyed. But they were happy and together. And, like the rest of the country, they entered their new lives under a new king.

⌒⌒⌒

This legend was well known in Chertsey, and was made into a play in 1816 by Albert Smith. If you go to Chertsey, the bell is now in St Peter's Church. You can also see a statue of Blanche, made by Sheila Mitchell FRBS, standing by Chertsey Bridge.

SIXTEEN

EDWY THE FAIR, AND THE DASTARDLY ST DUNSTAN

In our history there were seven Saxon kings – five of them young men who came to power whilst still in their teens, and all seven crowned at Kingston, at the Kings' Stone. You can see the Kings' Stone today, placed outside the Guildhall, with a monument to each king.

Athelstan was the second of the Saxon kings crowned at Kingston. Already a full grown man, he was very astute and married his four sisters off to the most powerful men in Europe: the King of France, the Emperor of Germany, Hugo the Great (Count of Paris) and lastly the Duke of Aquitaine. None of his sisters had a choice in the matter. Their role was purely to maintain and sustain the dynastic links and allies. Love did not enter into the equation.

Athelstan had a friend who was a friar, Dunstan, later to be a saint – but no saint in our story. He pretended to be adept at magic, so the story goes, and Athelstan came under his influence. Athelstan died in 940 and was succeeded by his half-brother Edmund, who was only eighteen. He did well in protecting and securing the lands, and was called Edmund the Magnificent. He had little to do with Dunstan – he had no interest in magic.

However, Edmund had one vice: he drank a lot, and he died suddenly in 946 – after only six years on the throne.

Edmund had two sons, but they were no more than babes in arms. The parliament – the Wittenberg – decided that the boys were too young to rule, so they were passed over in favour of Edred, their father's younger brother.

Edred was still only a teenager, but he knew his own mind. Meanwhile Dunstan (desperate to get back into royal favour) spread a story that a 'miracle' had occurred while he was Abbot at Glastonbury Abbey. Dunstan claimed that the Devil had come to tempt him, but he had taken the red-hot pincers from the forge where he was working and seized the Devil by his nose! The story travelled far and wide, and his reputation as a wise and holy man grew – for only a truly holy man would have the Devil trying to tempt him. Edred was troubled by illness and, reassured of Dunstan's holy and honest nature, called him to court to assist him. Impressed by his smooth-talking, Edred appointed Dunstan as the Royal Treasurer. Now Dunstan had the power that he craved.

Let us just say that there are stories of 'irregularities' in the management of the Royal Treasury, which meant that some of the public money was mixed up with Dunstan's. All quite simple to resolve, of course. Especially when Edred died after just nine years' reign.

In the meantime, Edmund's sons, Edwy and Edgar, were in Dunstan's care. They were kept to a strict regime more suited to a monk. The younger prince, Edgar, being of holy and thoughtful nature, was happy to accept this world view. But Edwy had a different outlook. With his faithful bodyguard Raewald assisting him, he would often escape to the house of his mother's cousin, and there experience more of the everyday pleasures of life – much better than the gruel and mundane diet of the practising monk.

At the house of his mother's cousin was the young Elgiva. She was very fair, and as she grew older she became more beautiful. With such limited access to the outside world, it was most natural that the young Edwy would form an attachment to Elgiva. But it was one that was frowned on by the Church and the law of the land. They were close cousins, and by the rules of the Church they were not allowed to have a relationship, much less marry. Nonetheless, Edwy found himself longing for Elgiva's company every second that he was apart from her, and he resolved to marry her one day.

How did Elgiva feel about Edwy? She was, after all, only a pawn in her family's machinations and positioning for power. She enjoyed his company; she looked forward to his visits; and, on the advice of her mother, kept herself a pure maiden.

The news of Edred's death was unexpected. Edwy was only fifteen, Edgar a couple of years younger. Edwy felt sure that the Wittenberg would now appoint him as heir. There was only one problem – Dunstan. Dunstan had begun to suspect that the young prince might not be living the austere life that had been set out for him. Edwy thus feared that the influential Dunstan might sway the Wittenberg to choose the God-fearing Edgar instead. But his fears were to no avail; he was appointed king.

The coronation ceremony was held in Kingston – then called Cyngestun – and Edwy was crowned king. He stood proud on the Kings' Stone and declared himself the protector of all the vassal kings of Scotland, Cumbria, Wales, Mona and the Hebrides, and the kings of the dependent states of Kent, Mercia, Wessex and East Anglia. The Archbishop of Canterbury, Odo, was there, along with all the high-ranking clergy, and Dunstan.

There followed a great feast and celebration. This was the first time that the new High King had spent any time with the other kings and clergy. They expected time with him and opportunities to have a few words privately; they expected to bond through feasting, the sharing of stories and carousing. Edwy, on the other hand, had only one thing on his mind. He slipped away to the rooms of Elgiva and her mother.

At first his absence was not noticed, but when it was – and it was prolonged – there begun a muttering and a grumbling amongst the kings and clergy. The new king was showing great disrespect for this new power community. Archbishop Odo grew furious at the absence of the king, and commanded Dunstan to bring Edwy back to the court. Edwy might be a sovereign, but he was acting like a child.

It didn't take long for Dunstan to find Edwy. He had placed his crown upon Elgiva's head, and his coronation robes had fallen to the ground as, shall we say, he indulged in the passion that he had for her. When Dunstan came storming into the room, Elgiva did not know where to look for blushing, and Edwy was in a state of disarray. Furious, Edwy stood up, demanding to know the meaning of the disturbance. Dunstan (who had himself turned aside all temptations of the flesh) was furious when he saw the partly clad girl, and told Edwy that his duty lay in the company of the vassal kings and the clergy, and that his absence was a less than kingly act.

Edwy's response was that he would rather lie in the arms of his true love than be in the company of old men, and that he would rather forfeit the kingdom. Dunstan was incandescent with rage, and, using the same strength that he had used to wrestle with the Devil, he seized Edwy by the collar and dragged him away from the chamber, back to the assembled company. Edwy felt humiliated by Dunstan, and greatly resented being treated like this. Although he greeted his lords with apologies, the damage had been done.

Within days, Edwy summoned Dunstan to him, and asked him for detailed accounts of the treasury. With the sudden death of the King, Dunstan was not prepared for a close examination of the accounts, and he refused, saying that the money had been entrusted to him by Edred, and it was only to Edred that he was accountable. This gave Edwy the leverage he needed to take his revenge, and he commanded the arrest of Dunstan on suspicion of stealing from the King's treasure. Dunstan fled to Ghent to the relative safety of a monk's cell.

Edwy then fulfilled his heart's desire by quietly marrying Elgiva, who promised her husband that she would love him until her dying breath. None of the vassal kings or the grey-headed clergy were invited to the celebrations, which went long into the night.

Archbishop Odo was furious that the King had shown so little respect for the Church by breaching its rules, and he could see his power and influence potentially disappearing. As soon as he heard of the wedding, he knew what to do. Their union was strictly prohibited, and Dunstan had made sure that Edwy knew that. With such a breach between the King and the laws of the Church and the state, Archbishop Odo announced that Edwy and Elgiva were to be excommunicated. This was a serious disgrace for the kingdom, and left the vassal kings and the dependencies uncertain how to deal with the disrespectful Edwy. Only Wessex had the favour of the King, and they supported him.

With such a divide in the land, and supported by Odo, Dunstan now returned to England. Archbishop Odo announced that Edgar was now king, and the kings of Mercia and Northumberland declared themselves for Edgar.

Edwy was furious and, with his allies beside him, decided to fight for his crown. Elgiva was sent to Winchester, deep in the safe territory of Wessex. Edwy took his army to St Albans, then Dunstable and Towcester. He planned to take a small force into the Mercian lands and put down any voice of insurrection. But alas, he was ill-advised, and his brother Edgar's men turned the tables on him. His troops were defeated and he fled back to Wessex to ensure the safety of his queen, Elgiva.

On his journey, he began to realise the full depth of his undertaking. His passion for Elgiva had blinded him, and even his supporters were asking him to set aside his queen. Their closeness through blood was forbidden by the Church and was against the law of the land. And whatever responsibilities Edwy had, as High King he must uphold the law of the land. Some say that in his despair Edwy cried out, 'Better to lose my crown and become a subject, with a subject's liberty to love.' But his closest advisors shook their heads, and reminded him that a law-abiding subject would never marry within the prohibited degree of family ties.

Elgiva, safe in Wessex, heard the news of her husband's defeat. Fearful for his safety and well-being, she left Wessex, intending to go to his side. Alas, she fell into the hands of soldiers who were sympathetic to Archbishop Odo. Believing that he was an honourable and God-fearing man, she came into his presence fearful but confident that no harm would come to her. But Odo was now a man fighting for his right to power. Before him he saw a woman whom he felt had bewitched the King, and taken him away from the path of service to the Church. Her beauty haunted him, and Odo knew that any man would fall for her beguiling presence and magnificence.

He turned and ordered his soldiers to hold her down and brand her face, so that it would become scarred and ugly. He put his hands over his ears so that he did not have to hear her screams. When she collapsed and was barely conscious, he ordered that his soldiers take her far away to Ireland and sell her there as a slave, so that she would not return to these shores. He was not going to suffer the guilt of the death of a queen. In the middle of the night, two of his men carried the bundle away from the archbishop's residence, to do as he requested.

When Edwy finally returned, he searched for Elgiva – but all that anyone knew in Wessex was that she had ridden out of the castle and had not been seen again. She hadn't told anyone, because she didn't want them to try to stop her, but the secrecy made whisper and rumour rife, and it was suggested that she had deserted her husband.

Broken-hearted Edwy, seeing his kingdom fall about him, then conceded and his marriage was annulled. Edgar was declared king of the lands north of the Thames; Edwy was king south of the Thames. But it was an uneasy alliance, and while the kings and brothers faced each other, the Church stood aside, its position secured. There were border scuffles between the two kingships, and the peace was precarious.

Then Edwy received a message. Elgiva, having been taken to Ireland as a slave, had been met with kindness and understanding; and the scars on her face, placed there by Odo, had been healed in the soft waters. The Irish had treated her with the respect a queen deserved, and would now support her return to these shores. She sent word of her return, and the potential support of an Irish army.

When Edwy learned of Odo's duplicity, he was furious. At the same time, he was convinced that the return of his love was a message from God, advocating his marriage and his right to be the High King.

Odo and Dunstan now realised that their positions, and their power in the Church, were in jeopardy. They arranged to intercept Elgiva at Gloucester. Again she was brought before Odo, but this time she feared greatly for her safety. Odo felt that only by her death would Edwy realise that God was against the marriage, and cease taking action against the Church. Still reluctant to inflict a death blow himself, he had her subjected to vile torture. The hamstrings in her arms and legs were cut so that she could not stand up, or support herself on her arms. She was left in acute torment, and took several days to die. Her screams travelled up the stairway to Odo's own chamber, and he beat his own breast, remembering her beauty and the desires that he had put to one side.

When news of her death reached Edwy, it seemed that the life in him was sucked out. He suffered the turbulence of extreme emotions and felt confused and alone, unsure who to trust. Amongst even his supporters there were mutterings that maybe this was God's judgement for his contempt of the ecclesiastical statutes.

In a rage, Edwy took up arms against his brother Edgar. There were border incursions and Odo was killed in one of the battles. But the heart of Edwy was broken; he was unable to keep his head and he took risks. He died in battle and was buried at Winchester.

Edgar was declared High King over all the land. He was crowned on the Kings' Stone and soon appointed Dunstan as the new Archbishop of Canterbury. There were no more questions to be asked about the treasury, as Edgar was a devout follower of the Church and submitted himself and his kingdom to the authority of Dunstan. Dunstan now had all the power he wanted, and no one to challenge him.

∽∾

There is little today to remind us of Edwy and Elgiva and their great love. Just the markers around the Kings' Stone, one for each of the Saxon kings. You can see this in the forecourt of the Guildhall in Kingston. But it's interesting how things from history can become part of our everyday lives. I used to work for Kingston Borough, and, when we turned our computers on in the morning, a message would come up to tell us which of the several computer servers we were on that day. It could be Athelstan, Edmund or even Edgar. They had been named after the Saxon kings.

SEVENTEEN

THE LOSS OF
NONSUCH PALACE

How easy is it to lose a royal palace? A palace that all of Europe looked on with envy and awe?

On a patch of land between Cheam and Ewell, a mansion was built in the late eighteenth century. You can still see it today. It is in the grounds of Nonsuch Park, and the local Friends of Nonsuch have been working to keep the house open. The Mansion House was decorated to reflect the former glory of Nonsuch Palace, which used to be somewhere on the same site. No one knew exactly where the palace had originally stood; all they had were folk memories that had been handed down – father to son, mother to daughter – of the magnificence of the palace. But it was not just the glory that was remembered; it was also the anger and resentment of some of the families that had been removed from the land when the palace was built. Old memories die hard.

It was October 1537. King Henry VIII held his baby son in his hands and swore by all the ancient Greek gods, and the one true Christian god, that he would give the future king the best possible start in life, allowing him to become the greatest king of the Tudors.

Henry already had plans to build the finest hunting grounds – close to Hampton Court, with good access into London via the river. But now he had an even better idea: to build the most glorious of palaces, to surpass all the kings of all the lands he had ever known, and most certainly to outrank the King of France, Francis I. It would be a domain of learning, with every nook and cranny showing his son how to be a king. It would be a palace to define his dynasty; to be an everlasting reminder of the strength and power of Henry Tudor and his son, Edward. That was the plan and the vision. What is it they say about the plans of mice and men?

Cuddington was an old Roman settlement close to Stane Street, a Roman highway. Unfortunately for the tenants of the village of Cuddington, Henry had his eye on it. He owned the lands at Banstead to the south and Richmond in the north. With Cuddington, he would have a clear path from Hampton Court to hunt to his heart's content. Of course, he wasn't going to just 'take' the land. He had surveyors inspect it and value it. The surveyors went into great detail about the quality of the mansion house that was already there, and how new it was. They didn't even mention the tenants' houses, or the church. None of them – surveyors, tenants or churchmen – had any idea that Henry planned to demolish everything in his way, and build a new palace instead.

Now, normally there would have been an outcry at the demolition of a church. But Henry had already started dissolving the abbeys and priories, seizing the land and monies for himself. After all, had he not demonstrated that he was at least equal to the Pope as a representative of God on earth? Thus he had already suppressed the priory at Merton, just down the road, which traditionally protected the church at Cuddington. He had also suppressed the priory in Ixworth, Suffolk, and thus had it handily available to give to Richard Codington – who owned the coveted land in Cuddington – in compensation.

So, where to find building materials for the foundations and walls? No problem! There was a disused priory up the road in Merton. Slightly used. One previous owner. The walls were quickly demolished and the bricks brought down to Cheam, where work started on the new palace. It was to be called Nonsuch, as 'none such could compare' in the whole of Europe. Henry brought in the best Italian designers and artists, even poaching a few from the King of France!

His plan was to have busts of the Roman Emperor, stucco friezes of the Greek myths, and statues of gods and goddesses – all the virtues and representations of the liberal arts. Wherever he looked there would be something for the future king to learn about leadership. Henry wanted the palace to look like the Troy described in ancient writings. He had a statue made of himself resting his foot on a lion, and there was even a maze in the gardens to remind him of Theseus in the labyrinth.

But there was one Greek god that Henry did not take so much notice of. A holy place is a holy place, and the random pulling down of a church does not go unnoticed. In Greek mythology, the goddess Demeter was so appalled by Erysichthon's destruction of trees in her sacred grove that she sent famine to dwell in his belly. He had an insatiable hunger and eventually destroyed all that he held dear. Henry had an insatiable hunger too … for power and glory. How would that serve him? Now, you might think that what happens next was retribution from the gods, but I cannot possibly say.

The main structure was finished in 1541, and it took another five years to finish the internal and external decoration. However, as the result of an accident, Henry increasingly suffered from pains in his legs and had to be carried everywhere in a litter. He only visited Nonsuch Palace three times before dying in 1547. The young King Edward had little interest in the place, and it was left to stand until he died in 1553, just six years later. When Mary came to the throne she despised it, and sold it to the Earl of Arundel in 1553.

The Earl adored the palace. He tried to follow the plans and intentions of King Henry in the decoration of the place, and installed fountains and statues in the gardens. He spent so much money that he virtually bankrupted himself. When Mary died without any children, it was Elizabeth who came to the throne. Suddenly the Earl's plotting and planning became evident. He wanted to woo the new queen, and make her his wife. In the summer of 1559 he held a party at Nonsuch to celebrate her ascension to the throne. The palace was to be the backdrop of his courtship and seduction of the young queen.

After supper in the banqueting house there was a masque, with drums and flutes that played all night long. During the day there was hunting, and another banquet and masque in the evening. This occurred every day of the five days Elizabeth spent there. When she left, the Earl presented her with a cabinet full of gold and silver.

The party was a glamorous success – as a party – and Elizabeth was sufficiently enticed by the place to keep returning to take part in the hunting. The Earl was ever hopeful that she might show him some favour, but Elizabeth was able to flirt and keep him at a distance at the same time. She had no intention of becoming someone's third wife, even if the other two were dead.

When it finally dawned on the Earl that Elizabeth had no romantic interest in him, he looked for another way to gain power. Lady Jane Grey had been named by Edward as his successor, but she had been executed by Mary after only nine days on the throne. Technically her successor would have been her sister, Lady Catherine Grey. The Earl of Arundel thus became embroiled in a plot to put Lady Catherine on the English throne.

His conspiracy, however, was soon rumbled and he was lucky to just be put under house arrest. Never one to miss an opportunity for power, he then associated himself with a plot to put Mary, Queen of Scots on the throne. Elizabeth must have had some kind feelings for him as, again, she allowed him house arrest at Nonsuch. Anyone else would have been sent to the block! When he died in 1592, his debts were so great that his son-in-law, Lord Lumley, could not afford the upkeep of the palace. Instead, he rather craftily sold the palace to Elizabeth, and offered to stay on as the keeper, which Elizabeth accepted.

Elizabeth became a regular visitor to the palace, spending so much time at Nonsuch that her despatches were brought down from London for her to deal with. On one occasion, her officers caught up with her outside of Cheam, and the business was so urgent that they had to use a nearby house to call a council meeting. That house was called the 'Council House' for some time, and is now known as 'Whitehall'.

Elizabeth allowed herself to have favourites, including the young Earl of Essex. Alas, he became cocky and planned to use his favoured position to overthrow her. He had been sent to Ireland to quell a rebellion, but had made a deal with the rebels instead. Riding back to London with his army, he intended to take power in England for himself. To his disappointment, he found that Elizabeth was at Nonsuch, so he left with just six friends supporting him, expecting his army to follow. He was not aware that his army had taken the Queen's absence as an ill omen, and had disappeared into the night. The Earl rode to Nonsuch and burst into the Queen's chambers, demanding to see her.

He was somewhat foolish in expecting to be able to overthrow the Queen. On the other hand, the security arrangements at the palace must have been a bit lackadaisical for him to have got in. But whatever his intentions, and however fond the Queen was of him, one thing she did not tolerate was being seen in a state of undress – minus make up, and, most importantly, minus her wig! He was doomed from the moment he saw her in all her apparent nakedness. With no delusions about the fancy boy, Elizabeth uncovered the extent of his deceit, and the young Earl of Essex was detained and eventually executed in 1601.

Elizabeth continued to enjoy the house until the day she came back from hunting at Banstead Downs to see, from a distance, what she thought was the palace on fire. Racing there with her cortège, she was most put out to find her courtiers amused by her panic. She had been deceived by the sun shining on the windows of Nonsuch and the brilliance of the decorations. Elizabeth was so furious and embarrassed at having made a mistake that she turned her horse towards Richmond Palace and never went back to Nonsuch again. She died later the same year. Henry VIII's hunger for power and fame for his dynasty died with her.

The palace passed to James I and he gave it to his wife, Anne of Denmark. Their son, Henry, Prince of Wales, found Nonsuch to be to his taste. Tutors were installed there to enable the young prince and his friends to learn the knightly arts of chivalry, fighting, horsemanship and courtly virtues. Lord Lumley kept a well-stocked library there, and Henry had the opportunity to develop as a proper Renaissance prince – just as Henry VIII had envisaged. Sadly, Prince Henry died of typhoid fever in 1612, and it was his brother, Charles I, who came to the throne in 1625. He granted Nonsuch Palace to his wife Henrietta, who used it as a refuge on many occasions over the coming years. Unfortunately, they were not good at paying local bills or the wages of staff, which had some dire consequences.

An estate labourer, perhaps disgruntled at not being paid, was working at Nonsuch Palace late one Saturday night during the Civil War when he saw 200 Cavaliers on horseback arrive and settle into local quarters. He scurried off to Kingston, betraying Charles by warning the Parliamentary forces. However, they did not listen to him, and the Cavaliers then rode into Kingston where there was much 'ringing of bells for joy'. But not for long.

With the death of Charles I, the Parliamentarians sold off Nonsuch in two parts – one half to the man who had been in charge of the Parliamentary forces, Major John Lambert, and one half to Colonel Thomas Pride, who had been a signatory to the death sentence of the King.

Nonsuch was neglected for the next few years and its glory faded. With the restoration of Charles II, his mother took back possession of Nonsuch and placed it in the charge of Lord Berkeley. During the Great Plague and the Fire of London, Nonsuch Palace was used to house the Exchequer, the money of the Kingdom, and the Royal Treasury, as it was a safe distance from London.

Once the Exchequer moved back to Westminster, Lord Berkeley took advantage of the absence of his royal mistress and began knocking down some of the buildings, including the grand banqueting hall, and selling them on as building materials. He was investigated, but, as the Crown had continued their habit of not paying wages and bills, Lord Berkeley blackmailed them with a list of their unpaid bills, and all of a sudden any investigation faded away. And he got paid too!

When Henrietta died in 1669, she passed Nonsuch back to her son Charles II. He had a mistress, Barbara Villiers, with whom he had a passionate affair and then discarded. She was a well-known gambler, having in one night gambled £20,000 (more than £1 million in today's money) and all her jewellery. Strapped for cash, she tried to extort money from Charles II. In return, he made her Baroness Nonsuch and gave her Nonsuch Palace. She soon recognised that it was a financial liability, and so she followed Lord Berkeley's lead. In 1682 a warrant was issued to allow the demolition of Nonsuch Palace, to be sold as building materials. First in line was Lord Berkeley, who used the material for the house he was building called Durdans.

Nonsuch Palace, built with a hunger for power, lasted less than 142 years. The destruction was 'probably the heaviest loss which English architecture has suffered since the dissolution of the monasteries'.

☙☙☙

Some people say that Nonsuch Park is haunted by shadowy figures and the sounds of merriment. Perhaps guests from one of the glamorous parties linger on. By the eastern gate of the park, there have been reports of a tall man in a black coat. Maybe it's the priest of Cuddington Church, searching for the faithful. The land was eventually owned by the Farmer family, and they built the Mansion House that stands there now. All signs of Nonsuch Palace and the site of Cuddington Church and village had been eradicated, living on only in folk memory. It was an archaeological dig, led by Martin Biddle in 1959, that finally uncovered the foundations of the palace and church. There is an exhibition, supported by the Friends of Nonsuch, in the Mansion House in Nonsuch Park, which details the history of this long-lost 'Pearl of the Realm'.

EIGHTEEN

A DISH FIT FOR A QUEEN

William the Conqueror was nervous. He was always nervous when it came to Matilda. She was only 5ft tall but she carried herself as the queen she was, and seemed a giant to him. A direct descendant of both Alfred the Great and Charlemagne, royal blood oozed through her veins. He knew he wasn't her first love and, when he had asked for her hand in marriage, she had laughed and said that she was too high born to marry a bastard. He had been furious. Technically he *was* a bastard – his mother and father had not been married – but he was the only male heir of his father and he had successfully made the case to take the title of Duke of Normandy when his father died.

He had won her round, and, with Matilda at his side, he controlled much of Northern France. It was she who encouraged him to think about the English throne when there was no obvious successor to Edward the Confessor. It was she who paid for a ship to add to his fleet to cross the English Channel. And it was to her that he entrusted the rule of the land in Normandy while he was establishing himself in England.

It was important to William that he be crowned King of England as soon as possible. He needed to establish his authority but he also wanted Matilda by his side, crowned as queen.

Of all his knights and companions, it was his wife he trusted most should he ever need to leave someone else in charge. She had done it in Normandy and he would need her to do it in England. He intended the coronation vows to confirm the importance of his consort. She too was to be divinely placed by God, sharing in the royal power and blessed by her people.

But to get her to come to England was difficult. She hated being on the sea and wasn't good at sailing. She had three children already, and a fourth one on the way. With the morning sickness, she really wasn't keen. Time was ticking on, and William wanted the coronation to take place during Pentecost. This religious festival, which celebrated the birthday of the Christian Church, had a special significance:

> And when the day of Pentecost was fully come, they were all with one accord in one place. And suddenly there came a sound from heaven as of a rushing mighty wind, and it filled all the house where they were sitting.
>
> Acts 2:1–2

William wanted his reign to be 'all with one accord' too.

Matilda had now agreed to suffer travelling across the sea to join him for the coronation. He appreciated her effort and wanted to give her something that would be suitable for a woman with a delicate stomach, yet also send a powerful message to his knights. He consulted Tezelin, his master chef whom he had brought from Normandy, who promised him a dish fit for a queen.

The coronation was held, and the knights and supporters made vows to both the new king and queen. However, some of the knights were uncertain about being overseen by a woman. She was so small. Could she take control of the country if William was absent? They shook their heads and muttered behind their hands.

And now to the banquet.

That's what made William nervous. Would Tezelin come up with something that would convey the message that one should not be deceived by first impressions? Would Matilda get the inference?

After all, her first impression of him had been so poor that she had thrown him aside – but had he not risen to the occasion, becoming king of both sides of the Channel? Would the knights understand the subtlety of the jest?

Tezelin brought forward the plain earthenware dish and raised the lid. Inside, the soup was white, plain and looked very unappealing. Matilda threw William a glance. Was this all he had for her, given the journey she had had to make for him?

William nodded. He took a spoon, dipped it in the dish, and then raised it to her lips. Cautiously she bent to sip from it, grabbed his hand, and then took another sip. She laughed. She clapped her hands with delight and then took another sip with her spoon. Soon everyone wanted a taste of this bland-looking soup that so delighted the Queen.

And she understood, as did everyone else that day, that even the blandest, most uninteresting-looking morsel might have hidden depths of flavour, taste and strength. Tezelin had made a soup that contained almond milk, brawn of capons, sugar, and chicken parboiled with chopped spices; it was absolutely delicious. He called it dilligrout.

William was so pleased, that he presented Tezelin with Edistone Manor at Addington, and announced that the Lord of the Manor of Addington would forever present such a soup to the monarch on the occasion of the coronation.

In the future, it was served up after the first course of the great coronation banquet in Westminster Hall. There was a very solemn procession, led by the Lord High Steward, Lord High Constable and the Earl Marshal of England, all three on horseback, and preceded and followed by the sergeants-at-arms with their maces. Next came the Treasurer and Comptroller of the Household, then the Sewer and Assistant-Sewer, and after them twenty-four gentlemen-at-arms bearing twenty-four dishes of meat. The Lord of the Manor of Addington, attended by two clerks of the kitchen in satin gowns, then appeared on the scene with his mess of dilligrout, and offered it to the King.

⌒⌒⌒

And that was what the Lords of the Manor of Addington did until the reign of George III. Apparently, by then the recipe had changed to a 'herb pudding boiled in a pig's caul', which doesn't sound so good. When Frederick English, a diamond millionaire from South Africa, took possession of Addington Manor in 1898, he applied to serve the dilligrout at the coronation of Edward VIII – but was turned down on the grounds that the custom had been discontinued.

By the way, dilligrout is also one of the passwords for the Gryffindor common room in the Harry Potter books.

NINETEEN

THE MYSTERY OF POLLY PAINE

Godstone is a pretty little village: a cluster of old houses, a village green and a pond. A pleasant place to live and one that has a history stretching back to Saxon times. No wonder there are so many stories about the place.

Just past Enterdent Road is an area known as Polly Paine Bottom. It's a funny name, to be sure, but a bottom in this case is a term for low-lying land next to a river, not a part of someone's anatomy! You can see the river on the maps, leading into Leigh Place Pond.

In the middle of the nineteenth century, an old woman called Polly Paine lived in a white house on the corner of Enterdent Road and what is now Eastbourne Road. She had been a travelling woman, and was regarded with suspicion by her neighbours. As she went from door to door selling her wares, several people in the back bar of the coaching inn would mutter under their breath about travellers and their strange ways.

Sometimes people would pass her in the road. She'd be searching in the hedgerows for herbs and leaves, maybe even a few berries in season. She was a little unkempt, and she would often be mumbling to herself. The people she had known had long gone, and she was known to the local children as Mad Polly Paine. Generally, she kept herself to herself.

One day a stranger to the village walked down the lane where her house was. He saw a cat on the side of the road and, being partial to cats, he picked it up. The cat struggled in his arms, trying to get away, just as any sensible cat would do. The more the stranger tried to keep hold of the cat, the more the cat struggled and scratched – getting bigger and bigger until the stranger had to let go as it was so big and heavy. As soon as the cat touched the ground and was free, it shrunk down to its original size, turned and spat at the stranger, and then disappeared. The stranger was shaken, and pretty well-clawed, so he made his way to one of the coaching inns in the village where he regaled the locals with tales of his fight with the incredible growing cat. He received sympathy from the barmaid for the wounds he had sustained. And at the back of the bar, knowing looks were exchanged.

One of the local farmers wanted to move his hayrick and take a short cut through the lane outside Polly Paine's house. She came out and shouted at him because he had blocked the road; but the farmer just shouted back louder, arguing that he would do as he pleased and there was nothing on God's earth that would change his mind.

Polly went back into the house, but minutes later a dog ran out the other side of the house through the hedge, in front of the horse. The dog kept out of the range of the hooves but made a lot of noise, and kept diving in to nip at the horse's ankles. The horse panicked and reared up on its hind legs, then tried to dash away from this nightmare. He was still attached to the cart with the hayrick, and, as the horse lurched away, the hayrick lost balance and the contents fell into the road. No one had ever seen this dog before and it was never seen again.

Polly Paine came back out of her house, smiled, and asked if there had been something on God's earth that had changed his mind. The farmer was in despair at his hay on the road and pleaded with passers-by to help him get his hay back on the cart. But one look from Polly Paine, and all of them passed on the other side of the road. Down at the coaching inn, in the back bar, heads nodded and knowing looks were exchanged.

The unspoken suspicion was 'proved' to be true one day when the hounds were out in the fields. They picked up the scent of a hare, and chased it down and around. The huntsmen on their horses were following, watching where the hare went. One of the hounds darted forward, stretched his neck that extra inch, and had the hare in his teeth. The hare twisted and turned, and the hound found himself letting go. There was blood on his lip. The hound reached again for the hare, but by this time they were almost at Polly Paine Bottom. The hare dived into the Stratton culvert, and the hounds lost their scent. The huntsmen cursed, searched the culvert, but could only find a smear of blood where the hare had disappeared. Then they turned and went back across the field looking for another hare to follow.

The next day Polly Paine was seen limping along the lane. No one knew what she had done to hurt herself, and she did not say anything to anyone.

Down in the coaching inn, those in the back bar nodded their heads. And now they knew beyond a shadow of a doubt that she was a witch and a shape-shifter. They knew she had never harmed anyone, but, just in case someone upset Polly again, some of the farmers put a piece of iron, or a stone with a natural hole in it, over their animals' stalls to protect them. Their wives placed an odd pin in the door, and the men kept a sycamore switch by the door to keep the witch out.

☙☙

Was Polly a witch and a shape-shifter? Did they need to take precautions? Or was it all just wild rumours about a person who did not fit in with the local community? Perhaps she got more respect after the incident, or maybe they just knew better than to mess with someone who had such amazing skills.

TWENTY

THE ROLLICKING HISTORY OF A PIRATE AND SMUGGLER

Back in the seventeenth century, young John Trenchman lived down by the docks in East London. He loved the smell of the spices, the sounds of the sailors calling out in different languages, and the taste of the strange foods that were passed to him as scraps to be thrown away. He loved listening to the stories told to him of distant places, and journeys where you could see nothing but the water for days at a time.

On a good day he'd have some work, unloading some of the ships, but his money was always snatched from his hand by his father. And in the evenings, John would have to bring him home from the pub to the room where they lived with four other men. At night John had dreams of escaping from the cramped, mouldy room, and the bad breath and putrid smells all around.

One day, at high tide, his father came towards him to take his money. A cargo ship was about to set sail, and the gangplank was just being pulled up. Something in John made him turn away from his father, take a run up, and, with a leap of faith, grasp the side of the ship as it pulled away. 'Sir!' he said. 'I want to be a sailor!'

There was laughter as the men on deck looked at the lad. He was big for his years yet still young. And they saw his father on the dock, dancing the rage of a man whose need for money for drink outweighed any concern for his son. The quartermaster remembered his own father, cuffed John behind the ear, and told him to take his muscle to the mainsail.

Handling sails and performing all the other duties of a boy sailor required a different kind of strength to unloading docks. And there were times below deck when John was sleeping in the company of four or five other sailors, and he would wake in the night and think himself back in that cramped, mouldy room with the bad breath and putrid smells all around him. But then he'd taste the salt still on his lips from the sea air, feel the movement of the ship, and know that he was far from London.

John learned his craft as a sailor quickly, and when he arrived in the Caribbean he was overjoyed by the heat. He knew he didn't want to return to England and the cold, the wet and the rain. He slipped ashore when the ship was preparing to return to England and hid until it had gone. It wasn't difficult to find another ship, and then another ship. Until the day that they were attacked by pirates.

A single shot was fired across the bow. That's all it took. The captain of John's ship surrendered and the pirates swarmed aboard to take the cargo and anything else they fancied. As long as the crew didn't fight back they wouldn't be harmed, and that's the way they liked it. Then the pirate captain came on board. He was like no one John had ever seen before, except for the fancy gentlemen who had stood in the harbour to collect their cargo. He was dressed in a velvet embroidered waistcoat, with lacy cuffs and a full wig topped with a tricorn hat. Really too fancy for words – and John had to stop himself from laughing. But when the pirate captain spoke of the pirate life and the promise of treasure for anyone who would join his crew, there was no question of who was in charge. When John thought back to all the times his father had taken the money he had sweated for, he decided then and there he would become a pirate.

He soon found that life as a pirate wasn't as exciting as he had hoped. The pirate ship was overcrowded – many men had decided that this was the life for them. There were also long periods of boredom spent waiting in sheltered harbours before they set out after a ship with promised treasure. As John lay in the cramped quarters, listening to the other pirates snoring in the night, he wondered what he had let himself in for. As a pirate, he was now outside the law.

When Captain Morgan came looking for men to join his attack of Portobelo in Panama, John stepped forward. Morgan was a good man to serve under. This privateer knew Portobelo well and how best to deploy his pirates. For fourteen days they fought, burned the city, and then released the prisoners kept by the Spanish – which included some high-ranking British nobility. Captain Morgan received ransoms of 250,000 pesos, and as much gold, silk and linen as he could get on his ship. John was well rewarded for his efforts. When Captain Morgan was summoned back to England, John travelled in the same ship. He had a hankering to go home and show his father how much he had achieved.

Captain Morgan was knighted by King Charles II for rescuing the nobles. John scoured the inns and lodging houses to find his father, but all he learned was that his father had drunk himself to death in an inn at the docks.

The call of the sea was strong, and John found himself on the south coast, working as a ship hand, grafting here and there. But his pirate ways stayed with him, and he looked for an opportunity to earn a bit on the side. Soon he was mixing with smugglers, who saw John as a safe and capable pair of hands. He could handle himself on the sea, and even better on land.

John would sail to the foreign ships, which were moored up to three miles out in the Channel. From these ships the men loaded their luggers and returned to shore. It took skill to manage a boat in the darkness, with no moon offering light. Men respected John and he became a leader of one of the work gangs. It was good work, as smugglers could earn in one night what they would earn for a whole week's toil in the fields. Indeed, farmers had to raise the wages during the harvest just to ensure that the men would stay on the fields rather than run to the smugglers' call.

John would send out a call that a consignment was coming in for the next moonless night. Some forty or fifty men would then gather on the shore at Bexhill. A signal was sent to the waiting ships in the Channel, and several luggers would pull out to meet the ships, where the tea, brandy and lace would be unloaded into tubs. Then they returned to the shore, all the time looking out to see if the warning flashlight or bonfire would come from the cliff tops. They had to be prepared for a visit from the revenue men, who would confiscate the contraband and arrest as many smugglers as possible. But not without a fight.

On shore, young men would haul the tubs of contraband from the luggers and load them onto the packhorses. Some of the horses were 'borrowed' from local farmers and would be returned in a somewhat exhausted and bedraggled state. Standing close by were the protectors. They were armed with wooden staves, swords or even firearms. They kept an eye out for the customs men. John still had his cutlass from his pirate days, and he cut a fine figure standing there – watching the sea for signals from the ship, overseeing the unloading and packing, and casting an eye to the horizon for any unwanted intruders.

They could unload as many as 500 tubs of contraband in twenty minutes – they worked fast and efficiently. Then the men split off into two groups, taking different routes to get into London.

From Bexhill, John would lead his gang through Hooe and Ashdown Forest. Resting there, they would part-bury the contraband in hollowed-out holes in the ground, covered with branches. If a local came across them during the day, they would mark a tub with chalk and leave quickly. They knew that if they took a tub, someone would come looking for them; but a marked tub would buy their silence. You see, there was a code of honour between the smugglers and the rest of the local community. Occasionally, the price was a tub of brandy, gifted by the smugglers in exchange for passing safely through the grounds of a grand mansion, or maybe taking shelter in a church. Each man had his part to play.

Up through Wych Cross and Forest Row they went, through East Grinstead, and to Godstone. From there into London. John was good at keeping his men safe and in order. His men worked together and protected each other.

That was until the day that Richard Cross, one of John's gang members, got himself into a brawl in a public house. He was found with contraband on him and was accused of being a smuggler. The authorities threatened to torture him into giving up the names of his gang. We don't know if he was tortured or if the threat was enough, but what we do know is that he told the customs men all the details of the next run.

While John was canny at varying his route in the dark, he would always come through Godstone, up by Tilburstow Hill. There was a clearing on the hill, just below the top. John would usually take his gang there for a rest, before moving on.

A week after Richard Cross was taken, the moon was dark and it seemed to be a good night for a run. The revenue men arrived during the day, and looked around at the oaks, ashes and larches, deciding which ones would afford the best views and the most cover. They climbed up into the trees, whilst others hid under the brambles and branches. And they waited.

John had no knowledge that anything was wrong. They had had a good run so far, and he was looking forward to counting out his share of the profits. But it wasn't a pleasant night – very cold and blustery. His cutlass was at his side and he watched and listened. It was as they came into the clearing that he realised something was wrong.

The owls hadn't been calling, and there was a different kind of smell. He heard a bramble branch bending, and started to call out

to his men. But too late. A firearm discharged and the man behind him tumbled to the ground. There followed shouts and cries as men reached for their own weapons – staves, swords and firearms. Smoke from the discharge, blood from the cuts, and splinters from the stave filled the air.

Determined to catch the smugglers, the revenue men had deployed twice their usual number, and the smugglers had no chance. John was shot in the shoulder and found himself knocked off his feet. He tumbled down the hill. He could hear the shouts, cries and moans of the living above him. He staggered to his feet, and made his way as best he could away from the revenue men. Despite all the years he had guided his men in the darkness, he no longer knew which direction he was going.

In the early morning, he stumbled into the courtyard of an inn, where he was found by the barmaid as she went out for some water. Her screams and cries for help brought out the landlord and the lad who helped with the horses.

They carried John into the bar and laid him on the table. They stripped off his outer clothes and gaiters, as they were covered with blood. The barmaid did what she could to bathe the wound. A doctor was summoned – but he had already had a visitor, and he arrived with three revenue men. They were too late. John had died on the table in the inn. His last words were, 'Just like my father', and then he was gone.

The residents of Godstone were horrified to hear of the battle just outside their village, and shocked that the last survivor had died in their local inn. They buried him in an unmarked grave outside the church, just as he was outside the law. 'Good riddance!' they thought.

Then strange things began to happen. Two gravediggers reported seeing a man in seaman's clothes standing behind the grave, disappearing as they approached. A stone which had been put on the grave was smashed to pieces. And fresh blood was found by the altar.

The people of Godstone were fearful that the ghost of John Trenchman had come back to haunt them, so they dug up his body and reburied him in the churchyard with a full Christian service. After that, there were no more reports of hauntings. Well, at least not in Godstone.

⌘

In the churchyard, by the main door, you can see the gravestone (with a skull and crossbones) where John was laid to rest.

Today you can visit the inn where he died. It's called the Fox and Hounds, and on the wall is a gaiter that they say has been authenticated as being 'typical of the ones worn by smugglers'. If you talk to the bar staff, they will tell you of ghostly goings-on in the pub, both in the day and night. The barmaid doesn't believe in ghosts, but she has heard footsteps in the room above the bar when no one else is around, and a noise from another room when no one was there. Glasses mysteriously fall from the top of a shelf above the bar, and appear on the shelf on the other side – by the whisky and the rum.

The barman will tell you of the time he saw a man dressed in old-fashioned clothes in the beer cellar, who faded away when challenged. They think it might be John Trenchman haunting the place where he took his last breath, enjoying a final drink.

TWENTY-ONE

RHYMES, A RIDDLE, POEMS AND A SONG!

This chapter is a bundle of rhymes which are particularly related to Surrey and contain elements of local folklore or sayings, so I make no excuse for including them!

RHYMES: SUTTON FOR MUTTON

Many folk rhymes describe certain characteristics of a place – be it the population or the local landscapes. Don't take these to heart!

> Sutton for mutton, Carshalton for beeves,
> Epsom for whores, and Ewell for thieves.

Another version says:

> Sutton for good mutton,
> Cheam for juicy beef,
> Croydon for a pretty girl,
> And Mitcham for a thief.

'Sutton for mutton' came from Sutton Common and the Downs, which afforded such splendid pasturage for sheep. Sutton Common has gone, enclosed in 1810, but the Downs remain. Alas, Sutton is no longer celebrated for anything above its fellow towns.

Riddle on the Letter H

Catherine Maria Fanshawe (1765–1834) was a poet and the daughter of a Surrey squire. This was written after a party in Leatherhead, where a guest bemoaned the poor attention that the letter H received.

'Twas whispered in Heaven, 'twas muttered in Hell,
And echo caught faintly the sound as it fell;
On the confines of Earth, 'twas permitted to rest,
And in the depths of the ocean its presence confessed;
'Twill be found in the sphere when 'tis riven asunder,
Be seen in the lightning and heard in the thunder;
'Twas allotted to man with his earliest breath,
Attends him at birth and awaits him at death,
Presides o'er his happiness, honour and health,
Is the prop of his house and the end of his wealth.
In the heaps of the miser, 'tis hoarded with care,
But is sure to be lost on his prodigal heir;
It begins every hope, every wish it must bound;
With the husbandman toils, and with monarchs is crowned;
Without it the soldier and seaman may roam,
But woe to the wretch who expels it from home!
In the whispers of conscience its voice will be found,
Nor e'er in the whirlwind of passion be drowned;
'Twill soften the heart; but though deaf be the ear,
It will make him acutely and instantly hear.
Set in shade, let it rest like a delicate flower;
Ah! Breathe on it softly, it dies in an hour.

Ballad: The Tunning of Elinor Rumming

I have heard this ballad by John Skelton (1550) described as 'a useful insight into the representation of aging women who ran their own businesses during the 16th century', or, alternatively, 'disgusting images of rural drinking and drunkenness'! Originally the pace was based on a liturgical chant, but it works very well if retold as a rap.

Tell you I will,
If that ye will
A-while be still,
Of a comely Jill
That dwelt on a hill:
She is somewhat sage
And well worn in age:
For her visage
It would assuage
A man's courage.
Droopy and drowsy,
Scurvy and lowsy,
Her face all bowsy,
Comely crinkled,
Wondrously wrinkled
Like a roast pig's ear,
Bristled with hair.
Her nose some deal hookéd,
And camously-crookéd,
Never stopping,
But ever dropping;
Her skin loose and slack,
Grained like a sack;
With a crooked back.
Jawed like a jetty;
A man would have pity
To see how she is gumméd,
Fingered and thumbéd,

Gently jointed,
Greased and anointed
Up to the knuckles;
Like as they were with buckles
Together made fast.
Her youth is far past!

And yet she will jet
Like a jollivet,
In her furréd flocket,
And gray russet rocket,
With simper and cocket.
Her hood of Lincoln green
It has been hers, I ween,
More than forty year;
And so doth it appear,
For the green bare threadés
Look like sere weedés,
Withered like hay,
The wool worn away.
And yet, I dare say
She thinketh herself gay
Upon the holiday
When she doth her array
And girdeth on her geets
Stitched and pranked with pleats;
Her kirtle, Bristol-red,
With clothes upon her head
That weigh a sow of lead,
Writhen in wondrous wise
After the Saracen's guise,
With a whim-wham
Knit with a trim-tram
Upon her brain-pan;
Like an Egyptian
Cappéd about,

When she goeth out.

And this comely dame,
I understand, her name
Is Elinor Rumming,
At home in her wonning;
And as men say
She dwelt in Surrey
In a certain stead
Beside Leatherhead.
She is a tonnish gib,
The devil and she be sib.
But to make up my tale
She breweth nappy ale,
And maketh thereof pot-sale
To travellers, to tinkers,
To sweaters, to swinkers,
And all good ale-drinkers,
That will nothing spare
But drink till they stare
And bring themselves bare,
With 'Now away the mare!
And let us slay care.'
As wise as an hare!
Come who so will
To Elinor on the hill
With 'Fill the cup, fill!'
And sit there by still,
Early and late.
Thither cometh Kate,
Cisly, and Sare,
With their legs bare,
They run in all haste,
Unbraced and unlaced;
With their heelés daggéd,
Their kirtles all jaggéd,

Their smocks all to-raggéd,
With titters and tatters,
Bring dishes and platters,
With all their might running
To Elinor Rumming
To have of her tunning.

She lendeth them on the same,
And thus beginneth the game.
Some wenches come unlaced
Some housewives come unbraced
Some be flybitten,
Some skewed as a kitten;
Some have no hair-lace,
Their locks about their face
Such a rude sort
To Elinor resort
From tide to tide,
Abide, abide!
And to you shall be told
How her ale is sold
To Maud and to Mold.
Some have no money
That thither comé
For their ale to pay.
That is a shrewd array!
Elinor sweared, 'Nay,
Ye shall not bear away
Mine ale for nought,
By him that me bought!'
With 'Hey, dog, hey!
Have these hogs away!'
With 'Get me a staffé
The swine eat my draffé!
Strike the hogs with a club,
They have drunk up my swilling-tub!'

Then thither came drunken Alice,
And she was full of talés,
Of tidings in Walés,
And of Saint James in Galés,
And of the Portingalés,
With 'Lo, Gossip, I wis,
Thus and thus it is:
There hath been great war
Between Temple Bar
And the Cross in Cheap,
And there came an heap
Of mill-stones in a rout.'
She speaketh thus in her snout,
Snivelling in her nose
As though she had the pose.

'Lo, here is an old tippet,
An ye will give me a sippet
Of your stale ale,
God send you good sale!'
'This ale,' said she, 'is noppy;
Let us suppé and soppy
And not spill a droppy,
For, so may I hoppy,
It cooleth well my croppy.'
Then began she to weep
And forthwith fell asleep.

'With Hey! and with Ho!
Sit we down a-row,
And drink till we blow.'

Now in cometh another rabble:
And there began a fabble,
A clattering and babble
They hold the highway,

They care not what men say,
Some, loth to be espied,
Start in at the back-side
Over the hedge and pale,
And all for the good ale.

'With Hey! and with Ho!
Sit we down a-row,
And drink till we blow.'

Their thirst was so great
They asked never for meat,
But drink, still drink,
And 'Let the cat wink,
Let us wash our gummés
From the dry crummés!'
Some brought a wimble,
Some brought a thimble,
Some brought this and that
Some brought I wot ne'er what.
And all this shift they make
For the good ale sake.
With Hey! and with Ho!
Sit we down a-row,
And drink till we blow,
And pipe 'Tirly Tirlow!'

But my fingers itch,
I have written too much
Of this mad mumming
Of Elinor Rumming!
Thus endeth the geste
Of this worthy feast.

Poem: The Fairies' Farewell

This poem, which contains references to some Surrey fairy lore, was written by Richard Corbet, who was born in Ewell and became Bishop of Oxford in 1628.

Farewell, rewards and fairies,
Good housewives now may say,
For now foul sluts in dairies
Do fare as well as they.
And though they sweep their hearths no less
Than maids were wont to do,
Yet who of late for cleanness
Finds sixpence in her shoe?

Lament, lament, old Abbeys,
The Fairies lost command!
They did but change Priests' babies,
But some have changed your land.
And all your children, sprung from thence,
Are now grown Puritans,
Who live as Changelings ever since
For love of your domains.

At morning and at evening both
You merry were and glad,
So little care of sleep or sloth
These pretty ladies had;
When Tom came home from labour,
Or Cis to milking rose,
Then merrily went their tabor,
And nimbly went their toes.

Witness those rings and roundelays
Of theirs, which yet remain,
Were footed in Queen Mary's days

On many a grassy plain;
But since of late, Elizabeth,
And later, James came in,
They never danced on any heath
As when the time hath been.

By which we note the Fairies
Were of the old Profession.
Their songs were 'Ave Mary's',
Their dances were Procession.
But now, alas, they all are dead;
Or gone beyond the seas;
Or farther for Religion fled;
Or else they take their ease.

A tell-tale in their company
They never could endure!
And whoso kept not secretly
Their mirth, was punished, sure;
It was a just and Christian deed
To pinch such black and blue.
Oh how the commonwealth doth want
Such Justices as you!

Song: Poor Murdered Woman

This was collected by Lucy Broadwood from a young labourer in Milford. Sadly this tale follows a theme that was all too common.

It was Hankey the squire, as I have heard say,
Who rode out a-hunting on one Saturday.
They hunted all day but nothing they found.
But a poor murdered woman, laid on the cold ground.

About eight o'clock, boys, our dogs they throwed off,
On Leatherhead Common, and that was the spot;
They tried all the bushes, but nothing they found
But a poor murdered woman, laid on the cold ground.

They whipped their dogs off, and kept them away,
For I do think it's proper he should have fair play;
They tried all the bushes, but nothing they found
But a poor murdered woman, laid on the cold ground.

They mounted their horses, and rode off the ground,
They rode to the village, and alarmed it all round,
'It is late in the evening, I am sorry to say,
She cannot be removed until the next day.'

The next Sunday morning, about eight o'clock,
Some hundreds of people to the spot they did flock;
For to see the poor creature your hearts would have bled,
Some odious violence had come to her head.

She was took off the coffin, and down to some inn,
And the man that has kept it, his name is John Simms.
The coroner was sent for, the jury they joined,
And soon they concluded, and settled their mind.

Her coffin was brought; in it she was laid,
And took to the churchyard that was called Leatherhead,
No father, no mother, nor no friend, I'm told,
Came to see that poor creature put under the mold.

So now I'll conclude, and finish my song,
And those that have done it, they will find themselves wrong.
For the last day of Judgement the trumpet will sound,
And their souls not in heaven, I'm afraid, won't be found.

THE TRIAL OF JOAN BUTTS, SO~CALLED WITCH OF EWELL

Many of the men who fought in the Civil War died on the battlefields, leaving their wives, children or sweethearts alone. As the widows grew older, they learned to deal with their grief as best they could.

For a woman alone it was a difficult time, and it was hard to make ends meet. Sometimes working as a servant; sometimes having to beg from door to door. Joan Butts of Ewell was such a woman. No one could remember if she had ever had a husband, or if she had any children. There was no one to help her or support her. But she was always ready to help out, look after a sick child, or provide cures for an ailment.

One day she heard that young Mary Farborough had been taken ill. The young girl twisted and turned, cried out, and was most violent with her fists and feet. Neighbours were convinced that the child was under a spell. The doctor was sent for, but he had little training and didn't really know what he was dealing with. Instead he decided to agree with the neighbours, and confirmed that Mary was indeed bewitched. He told her parents to save some of her urine, stop it up in a bottle and bury it, and then burn her clothes.

This would ensure that the witch was found out, as they would be drawn to the house and suffer the same ailments as Mary. It was a well-known precaution, he said, and once they knew the culprit, Mary would be restored to good health. Otherwise there was nothing he could do. Thus the urine was collected, bottled and buried. The maidservants were sent to burn the clothes in the garden.

Then Joan Butts arrived at the door. She was dishevelled, and looked absolutely ghastly. She said she had had a similar illness herself the past seven weeks, and, learning of Mary's illness, had come to offer comfort. There was a particular potion which she had found to be useful, and she wanted to suggest it to young Mary.

But as she stood there speaking, she threw down her hat and collapsed in a fit of twisting, turning and crying, lashing out with her fists and feet. Mary's parents were not sure what was happening. Was this the witch who had put a spell on their daughter? Had burning the clothes revealed her as the enchanter? When the fits abated, Mary's shaken parents showed Joan the door, unsure what else to do. The potion didn't help Mary, and a week later she died. Then the rumours began to circulate about Joan, and people started to treat her with suspicion.

Joan Butts struggled on. The day after Mary died, she called at the house of a Mr Tuers. She was begging for a pair of gloves, or something to keep her hands warm. It was cold and she had no money. He wasn't in but his maid, Elizabeth Burgiss, a young slip of a girl, told Joan in no uncertain terms to leave and not bother the house. Joan turned away, but came back again. She was desperate. If not gloves, then perhaps a pin to secure her neck cloth to keep out the cold? Begrudgingly Elizabeth gave her the pin, just to get rid of her.

But you know how thoughts come into your head. Thoughts that are difficult to shift. Thoughts that take you down one track until you find you can't get away from them. That's what happened to Elizabeth, who had heard the rumours about Joan. As she closed the door on her, she suddenly realised something. She had probably just upset a witch. She had heard all the tales of witches and demons – they always made those who crossed them pay a price. Elizabeth knew what she herself was like. If someone upset her, well, she would try to get her own back somehow. How would a witch like Joan get at her?

Elizabeth decided to stay in the house and garden. That would be safest, she assured herself. But over the next few days she was certain that stones were being pelted at her – falling on her clothes and in her hair, both inside the house and out. When she turned to see who had thrown them, no one was there.

The doors of the house kept opening and shutting, hitting only Elizabeth as they did so. She felt herself being pricked in the back, and a great pain came over her. She began to scream and shout, pleading for help. Her master, Mr Tuers, and his friend, Mr Waters, found her in a heap in the kitchen, begging for relief. Bewildered, Tuers offered to reach down the back of her dress to find the cause of her pain. He stretched his hand under her clothes and declared that he had found a lump of clay with pins in it; he 'threw' this into the fire. Elizabeth initially seemed relieved, and then started screaming again. Waters, not wishing to be outdone, then also reached under her clothes. He declared that he had also found a lump of clay, this time with thorns in it, that he too 'threw' into the fire. Only then did she calm down.

Elizabeth was convinced that she was under a curse, but her master would have none of it and urged her to continue her duties instead. Reluctantly she went out to milk the cows, passing by Nonsuch Park. There she saw Joan Butts in such a wet and bedraggled state that she convinced herself Joan had been 'lately conferring with some infernal fiend'. She was sure that Joan had been talking with the Devil about more ways to torment her. All for the sake of a pin reluctantly given!

She ran home to her master, claiming that Joan Butts was a witch and declaring everything that she had seen. Her master was still reluctant to make accusations, and again he urged her to continue her duties.

Later that day, Elizabeth went into a room to fetch a trunk that was to be sent to London. She screamed and cried out for her master, who came running. Elizabeth claimed that Joan had been in the trunk, although there was no one to be seen.

She also claimed that the andirons, the metal supports for the logs in the fireplace, had once been thrown at her, and all her linen had been thrown about. She claimed that a wooden bar had come off the door and flown across the room. The bellows, she said, had flown about the room and the pewter candlesticks had been thrown at her as she worked in the house. Elizabeth was becoming hysterical.

Completely out of his depth, and not one to believe in curses, Mr Tuers suggested that Elizabeth go home to her mother and father in Ashtead, about three miles from Ewell. It would give him some relief, and she might find some comfort from her mother. But as she walked down the road, Elizabeth was sure she was showered by acorns and stones.

She finally reached her mother's house, but there was to be no relief for her there. Strange things continued to happen. Her grandfather's britches were found on the top of the house, near enough over his bed. No one knew how they got there! And the pewter plates and dishes danced around the house, and even hit a visitor in the back. Each person felt that they had to dance to the Devil's own tune, to avoid being hit. A fiddle was also mysteriously moved – to the wall, then to the top of a bed – and finally it disappeared and was not seen again.

Elizabeth's mother, Mrs Burgiss, was worried for her daughter. She had heard the story and had seen things happen. There was clearly no other answer. Her daughter was cursed, and the most likely sorceress was Joan Butts. As far as she was concerned, all the evidence fitted together.

Elizabeth went back to her master's house. Things had calmed down there, but Elizabeth was always looking over her shoulder, always prepared in case something else was thrown at her.

Later that week there was a fair at Ewell, and Mrs Burgiss went to sell her wares. It was there that she saw Joan Butts. Possessed with an overwhelming desire to protect her daughter from this witch, Mrs Burgiss attacked Joan. It was reported that she 'so evilly treated [Joan] that [she] fetched out some of her hellish hellish [*sic*] blood'. The women were separated and charged with brawling in a public place. But Mrs Burgiss was so insistent in her accusations that the authorities began to take notice.

Despite it being Mrs Burgiss who initiated the attack, once the evidence was considered it was Joan who was taken – on a charge of witchcraft. Joan was bewildered and cried out that she had not bewitched Mary Farborough, but 'if all the devils in hell could helped [*sic*], she would bewitch her'. Alas, this compassion for Mary was taken as evidence of Joan's involvement with the Devil, even though she declared that she meant no such thing. Joan was indicted on two counts of bewitching Mary Farborough to death, and was accused of using witchcraft to torment Elizabeth Burgiss.

In March 1682, Joan appeared before Lord Chief Justice Sir Francis Pemberton at the court in Southwark. The session lasted three hours, with twenty witnesses called – all of them were against her, accusing her of being a witch and citing all kinds of examples. Today, if a cow's milk turned sour, we might think that the animal was ill or the milk had been left out too long; but at this time, people were quick to lay the blame on Joan if she had been anywhere near the cow. Joan did herself no favours, as she cast aspersions on some of the witnesses, accusing one witness of being in league with the Devil, having given himself 'body and soul'. Sir Francis Pemberton asked her what her evidence was for this accusation, but Joan mumbled and could give no reply. Her fate hung in the balance.

Timing was everything. The taste and flavour for witch-hunts had been dying out in England. During the Civil War the witch-hunts had been extreme, with no overall authority to rein them in. Impassioned men could assign themselves witch-hunters, and people with little power could assert themselves briefly by making accusations and giving evidence. With the Restoration came order, and a new way of thinking. Sir Francis Pemberton was a man of integrity, and a man of the new scientific world. He wasn't convinced by superstition.

He listened to all of the evidence, and then let common sense prevail. Joan was acquitted of all charges. Sadly, it was difficult for her to go back to her home in Ewell. Despite having been acquitted, there were still suspicions about her every movement. The enlightenment of her judges had not reached Ewell. Once the words that branded her a witch had been spoken aloud, it was difficult to rescind them. There were still whispers behind her back, and to her face, and she was treated with great distrust. She was not wanted here. In the end she went on the road, facing the fates and the fickleness of the weather until the day she died.

Elizabeth fared much better. She met a young man called William Williams, and married him four years later. We don't know what happened to them, but we can only hope they lived a long and full life of tolerance and understanding, together in compassion and companionship, unlike the life of Joan Butts.

TWENTY THREE

TROUBLESOME
BULLBEGGARS

Watch out if you go down the road in the night.
The Bullbeggars are out, and you'll take fright!

Once upon a time the Bullbeggars had the run of Surrey. They could go wherever they wanted – no one could hold them back. Were they a beast? Some kind of fairy? Whatever a Bullbeggar was, it could spring across the road and snatch you away, taking you no one knew where! Some people said the creatures were the result of burying two people in one grave. With not enough room, their bodies would cross over and their souls would merge to create a Bullbeggar. If you managed to kill one, the bogy beast would revert back to two bodies. They congregated around graveyards – some say to protect the dead, others say to feast on their bodies. Bullbeggars were tricky characters, and if they got into your house and they didn't like you, they would throw all kinds of things about.

Today in Woking there is a Bullbeggars Lane. It was originally a pleasant country path – with an open secret. Bullbeggars lived there! A farmhouse there was known to be inhabited by Bullbeggars, who threw all sorts of household goods around, and generally created mayhem and havoc. Things would get lost all the time. A pitcher of milk would be left on the table, but when the farmer's wife turned to use it, it would be gone. No matter how much she searched, she couldn't find it. Yet when her husband came home, he only had to ask 'Why would they want a pitcher of milk?' and there it would be, on the sideboard. A place that she had checked countless times. Very frustrating.

Everybody else kept their distance; they didn't want the Bullbeggars staying with them. Over time, the owners of the house learned how to live with the Bullbeggars, but they had to be very careful not to upset them. The Farm became known as Bullbeggars Farm, and, as the lane developed, it became Bullbeggars Lane. The farm is still standing, but has another name now. All around it is a housing estate. It must be very different to the peaceful rural lane it used to be.

⌒⌒⌒

But you never know where you might find a Bullbeggar. While researching this story, I stood outside the old farmhouse and wondered aloud where the Bullbeggars might be. Bullbeggars, Bullbeggars where are you? For some reason I said it three times, and then went home.

During the next few weeks I kept losing things – cameras, maps, books. I was most unhappy, and wondered again (I should stop wondering) if it had anything to do with the Bullbeggars. Maybe I had said the charm that brought them home with me.

A fortnight later, I went for a research visit to the other place in Surrey called Bullbeggars Lane, in Godstone. This lane is quite close to a church. Leafy green. Some houses, but not too many. And at the end of the lane are two plague pits. One was known as the men's pit, and the other as the women's pit. In fact, ideal Bullbeggars land! I invited any Bullbeggars that might have travelled with me to take up residence in this place that was much more suited to their needs. And now, although I still lose things, it's nowhere near as much! I just hope the people of Godstone haven't noticed any peculiar new neighbours!

TWENTY FOUR

THE WILD
CHERRY TREE
AND THE NUTHATCH

This is my retelling of the version collected in Surrey by Ruth Tongue, a Somerset folklorist.

When the world was new and all the creatures were finding their feet, wings and fins for the first time, they were also trying out the different kinds of food. The deer liked to strip the bark from certain trees. The carp and minnows settled on weed in the streams. The birds preferred to eat nuts and berries.

Now, the trees and plants enjoyed all this attention, and vied to produce the best food. The animals, birds and fish were also jostling amongst themselves to get the finest food. And I have to say, some of the bigger, bossier animals claimed the best, sharing it only with their own kind.

Amidst all of this, the wild cherry watched on. She had the most beautiful red cherries, but the birds and the squirrels would try them, find them too bitter, and then spit them out. 'Eugh,' they said. 'Too bitter for us. Let them rot on the trees.'

The other trees laughed at her and told her she was no good. That saddened the wild cherry and she became very shy, trying to hide herself away behind a veil of white blossom.

Meanwhile, the nuthatch had a problem. He was small and nimble, running up and down tree trunks, nipping in and out of the branches and leaves, not minding whether they were downside up, or upside down. But he was dreadfully worried. He had no food of his own to eat.

The trees had turned red, orange, yellow and brown. It was autumn, and all the creatures were aware of winter approaching. What would they eat then?

The squirrels took refuge in the walnut tree. The wood pigeons roosted in the chestnuts. The woodpeckers laid claim to the filberts, and the field mice and thrushes were tussling over the cobnuts.

The nuthatch rather fancied the pine cones, but the tiny gold-crested wrens also liked them. The nuthatch was big enough to scare the wrens off, but he knew that the wrens would find it hard to find something else their small beaks could manage. The nuthatch wasn't a bully.

The wild cherry felt sorry for the nuthatch. 'I'm sorry,' she said. 'You are welcome to eat my cherries, but I know they can be bitter and the stones get spat out.'

'Ah,' thought the nuthatch. 'There are stones inside the cherries! Maybe that's it! I have got a good beak for breaking into seeds and fruit stones. Maybe if the flesh is too sharp, it will stop the other animals from eating them, and I can have the cherry stones for myself and other nuthatches! Thank you, wild cherry. You can be our winter pantry!'

At this, the wild cherry bristled with pride, and at last she began to stand tall.

TWENTY FIVE

THE PHARISEES OF TITSEY WOOD

In Titsey, near Oxted, there is a small cluster of woods – Titsey, Clacket, Square and Church Woods. Each of the other names make some sense – but Church Woods? There is no record of there ever being a church there, nor evidence that the land belonged to a church. But there is a story about a church that could not be built ...

Once, in the mists of time, the Pharisees played in Titsey Woods. They would emerge in the twilight at the point when the green of the leaves and the green of the grass change their shade in the setting sun. The birds would sing their evening chorus, and the Pharisees would dance betwixt and between the rays of the sun, as though playing with a giant maypole.

It was a sight that few people had ever seen, but the goodwives of Titsey knew the signs and were always ready. They would stop their work and creep out to watch the Pharisees dance. Their daughters were impatient to join in, and only the most sensible were allowed to attend, in case they created a disturbance. This, after all, was the Pharisees' time. Nobody wanted to harm them. This was a woman's secret, and the knowledge of the Pharisees was handed down from mother to daughter. If any of the boys saw the fairies, the memory of it faded as they grew older.

As the last rays of the sun faded away, the Pharisees would make their way to one of the nearby houses to play in the warm embers of the fire. If the house was neat and tidy, and the goodwife left out a bowl of water, then the Pharisees would leave a silver sixpence. Such good luck! But if they didn't like what they saw, then all night long the poor woman of the house would have to suffer the Pharisees pinching her. In the morning she would wake up black and blue. It was quite a challenge to keep the Pharisees happy, and more so if you didn't know when they would visit. So you always had to keep the house in good order.

Over time the settlement grew into a village, and there was a move to build a new church to celebrate the Christian god. It was the menfolk who wanted it, and the menfolk who planned it. Sadly, they didn't discuss it with their womenfolk. That was their first mistake. Their womenfolk might have warned them of the folly of their ways, because the men made a crucial second mistake. They started to build the church in the very field where the Pharisees gathered for their dance.

The land was cleared and foundations were laid. The women watched and waited, not sure what would happen. Slowly, the walls were built. Just a few inches from the ground, but enough to trip over if you didn't look where you were going. Twilight fell, and the green of the leaves and the green of the grass changed their shade in the setting sun. The men went back to their homes, exhausted.

There was such a screeching and howling that night. No one knew quite what it was, but in the morning every man, woman and child in the village was covered in small pinch marks. The men were confused – was this some infestation of bugs, or demons visiting in the night? The women watched warily; they knew it was the Pharisees.

The men returned to their work on the church, but were astounded to see that every part of it was razed to the ground. The foundations were there, but all the walls had been knocked down, stone by stone. Had some big animals wandered through in the night? Was that the cause of the noise?

Again the men tried to build the church walls, and again they returned the next day to find that the walls had fallen. Their nights were spent tossing and turning from the 'bites' of the bugs, and they were woken by the screeching and howling.

After six days of this, the men did not know what to do. They called a meeting of the entire village and told them what was happening. One of the goodwives stood up. 'I know what is happening!' she said. The other goodwives looked at her in horror. Was she going to reveal the mystery of the Pharisees? They held their breath.

'I had a dream,' she said. 'I saw men and women with wings come to the field.'

The women thought 'Pharisees!'. The men thought 'Angels!'.

'They walked around the village and then said that the best light of the sun falls in the far field, and that would be for the righteous.' She looked around. 'I wonder what that means.'

One of the men was quick to interpret for her. He could 'understand' what she, a mere woman, could not. 'It means that we have tried to put the church in the wrong place. God has shown us the error of our ways. The sun shines on the righteous, and we shall build the right house for God.' With that, the plans were made to start building again, but in a different field.

The women relaxed. Perhaps now everything could return to normal.

Alas, there are some things that, once started, cannot be undone. The Pharisees tried to return to their dancing grounds, but the foundations were too solid. The land had been spoiled, and no matter how hard they tried, they could not turn it back to the way it had been. Instead they continued to shriek and howl, and pinch their way through the night. Their children were too scared to sleep.

The women held a meeting; they were a little frightened and anxious, and not sure how to deal with the problem. Finally they went to see the oldest woman in the village, the henwife. She knew all about the Pharisees, even though she wasn't able to creep along the forest floor to watch them any more.

'The foundations of the church have upset the balance. The Pharisees can't keep away because this is their natural habitat, but they can't stay here because the land has been sanctified against them. We need to find a way to create a balance between the angels and the Pharisees.'

'But what can we do?'

'What we do best. Use the plants to create a balance, so that neither the angels nor the Pharisees take precedence.'

They planted clematis (old man's beard), as it seemed to sum up the dilemma. On the one hand, the Pharisees claimed the white feathery fronds to play with; on the other hand, the angels told how those same fronds had offered shelter to the Virgin Mary and Jesus in their flight to Egypt. The women hoped that the enchanter's nightshade would bring about a union of opposites and resolve the conflict between the angels and Pharisees. Finally, they chose the yellow archangel that belongs to the dead nettle family. It doesn't have a sting, and, as with all nettles, it was known to protect against spirits and spells.

And it worked. The Pharisees weren't seen again and the children no longer awoke in the morning with black and blue marks on their bodies. However, the women had mixed feelings. One of their secret mysteries had gone. Such is the price of progress.

◌◌◌

There definitely isn't a church there. They gave up trying to build it in the face of such supernatural opposition. There are stories of a farmer who tried to plough the land, coming across the old foundations of a building. He decided that he would avoid that area, just in case the Pharisees came back. He had heard the stories!

Today that whole area is protected from anyone building on it. It's a Site of Special Scientific Interest. There are numerous interesting oak, ash, hazel and elm trees. Several rare butterflies and moths can be seen, and the undergrowth and flowers can be quite spectacular – with bluebells, plus delights such as old man's beard, the yellow archangel and enchanter's nightshade. There are even three kinds of orchid.

Just down the road is a service station on the M25. It was originally going to be called Titsey Services, and, because of the beauty of the locality, there was a lot of initial opposition to it being built. Fortunately, it's far enough away not to disturb the balance. For some reason they changed their minds and called it Clacket Services instead!

As I said, a very special place where the battle of opposites continues today.

TWENTY-SIX

THE
UPSIDE DOWN MAN

How many times have you wondered at the world, and thought it was so messed up that you would never understand it?

☙

Once upon a time there was a boy called Peter Labelliere. His family had been Huguenot refugees from France, and they had moved from place to place, never really settling anywhere. His father had died when he was young, and his mother took him to Ireland. The people spoke differently there, and his mother spoke her native French. He had to keep three languages in his head, and sometimes it felt like his world had gone topsy-turvy. But knowing three languages helped when he grew older. It helped him to think quicker. He became a pupil teacher in his school, and then progressed to being an assistant teacher. He soon learned to keep the unruly boys in hand, as they tried to turn things upside down.

He wanted to do well, and decided to join the Marines. He was sent off to the Americas, where he fought bravely to bring the colonies back under the control of the UK. But those pesky colonials were determined to have their independence. The British were no longer the leaders that they had been in the world.

☙

Peter rose up the ranks to become a major, and he became a close friend of the Duke of Devonshire. A poor boy such as he, best friends with a duke? Wasn't that the world turned upside down? If only his mother could see him now. When they both retired from the Marines, the Duke was pleased to award Peter a pension of £100 a year. A mere trifle to the Duke, but a fair fortune for an ordinary man to live on.

Now that he was well set up to support a wife and family, Peter soon became enamoured of a certain young lady, Hetty Fletcher. She lived in Cornwall, and he had met her when she was in London for the season. He usually found it difficult to speak to young women, but was surprised at how relaxed he felt in her company. She laughed at his attempts to make jokes, and seemed to be interested in him and what he had done. He believed that she reciprocated his affections and contemplated asking her to marry him. Encouraged by his friend, the Duke of Devonshire, he decided to ask for her hand in marriage at the last ball of the season. He was very anxious; his hands were sweating and his legs were shaking. Nonetheless, he stood before her and her friends, and he went down on one knee, and proposed. There was silence, and he could hear the beat of his own heart drumming in his ears as he waited, with bated breath, for her answer.

'No, I cannot marry you.'

He was sure that he had misheard, but, when he looked up at her, she had already turned away from him, followed by a gaggle of her friends, who were laughing and tittering. Feeling shamed and humiliated, he left the ballroom and never went back to that life.

Peter started to neglect himself, and shambled around the streets in his long blue coat, gilt buttons, knee breeches and worsted stockings. He became very outspoken, and would write political pamphlets raging at the injustices in the world. He would try to hand them out to passers-by. Small boys would chase after him to pick his pockets, and then be disappointed to find nothing but pieces of paper.

He moved away from London – away from his humiliation – to Dorking, where he took a room in an area known as the Hole in the Wall. Ever a generous man, Peter once took the coat off his back to give to a beggar who was cold. He felt strongly about the mistreatment of political prisoners, and even wrote to the King in protest, using his own blood as ink. He would talk about the most extraordinary things, and told everyone who would listen that one day carriages would run without the need of horses. How could that possibly happen? People began to shake their heads, and called him eccentric. But he lived through his personal motto: 'Freedom with God as my guide.'

Peter used to go for long walks on Box Hill. Standing at the top, and looking down over the countryside, he would gasp at the simplicity and beauty of it. The box bushes and yew trees covered the hill and he would sit for hours, drinking in all the scents and smells. He especially liked to sit in a thunderstorm, with the lightning and rain lashing around him. One night he was out very late when the storm came. He was soaked through and tried to make his way back to his lodgings in the downpour and darkness. He tripped over the undergrowth and fell; a single branch from a tree caught him in the eye and gouged it out. He staggered back to the house clutching his eye, with the blood running down his hands. He had lost his clear vision, and could only squint at the world.

On 6 September 1799, just after his seventieth birthday, he went for a walk on the hills. He was gone a very long time and his landlady was worried about him. When he finally returned, his coat was missing and he looked as though he had been in a struggle with some man or demon.

'The Devil,' he said. 'I met the Devil on top of Box Hill. He's coming back to collect my soul at 4 p.m. on a Friday in seven months.'

Nobody took much notice of him, and only the landlady saw how he became even more of a recluse, hiding himself away. One morning, as she took him in some breakfast, he grabbed her wrist and said that when he died, he wanted to be buried upside down with his feet above his head. The landlady shook him off and told him not to be so morbid. But he said again that his whole life had been so topsy-turvy that he wanted to be buried that way. His name was Peter, and he would be buried as St Peter had died.

On another occasion, he gave the son and daughter of the land-lady a coin each to dance upon his grave. Both children took his money, and then laughed at this strange one-eyed man in their home. But he took down a Bible and made them swear to do it. That frightened them.

No one else paid any attention to the prophecy but, just ten months later, at 4 p.m. on 7 June 1800, he died suddenly of a heart attack.

His funeral was well publicised, and some say that 3,000 people came to see this man being buried head-down in a verti-cal grave. The coffin was drawn up the hill on a hearse led by four black horses. A 10ft-deep hole had been dug. The coffin was placed in the grave and two men held it upright; the ground around it was packed with some of the chalk mud, until the coffin could stand by itself. The burial rites were spoken, and there was an opportunity for many to pay their last respects by throwing in soil.

It was such a spectacle. There were two cartloads of branches from yew trees and box trees. People used them to fan themselves in the heat, and then dropped them into the grave. The gravedig-gers then filled the grave and stood back. The landlady stood there with her two children. 'Go on,' she said. 'You took the money, now dance on his grave.'

The girl hid her face in her mother's skirts, but the boy leaped enthusiastically onto the grave and danced a jig all around. That set the tone for the rest of the company, and there was singing, laughing and dancing into the early evening.

Peter Labelliere did not lead a conventional life, and some might say he was mentally deranged, but his world was forever topsy-turvy. His plans to be buried this way meant that when the last judgement came, and the world was turned over, he'd have a fighting chance to be first out of the grave, and avoid that soul-seeking Devil.

There is at least one other person in Surrey alleged to have been buried upside down (at Leith Hill) and another two over in Sussex, all about the same time. Historians are of the view that only Peter Labelliere was really buried this way, and that the legends were attached to the others as an afterthought.

TWENTY SEVEN

THE BUCKLAND BLEEDING STONE

THE WHITE LADY

An eternal story of love and betrayal haunts the highways and byways of Buckland.

☜☞

One day, the pretty young daughter of a yeoman of Buckland caught the eye of the Lord of the Manor's son. Her father warned her of the duplicity of such men and tried to arrange a marriage between her and someone of a similar status. But she was headstrong and would have her own way.

When the young man saw her walking down the country lanes, he lost no time in muttering sweet nothings. She was flattered by his words of admiration and had her head turned. When he kissed her for the first time, her body thrilled to his touch, and she convinced herself that all his words were true blessings. But she was afraid of her father, and she swore the young man to secrecy about their meetings. The young man encouraged her deception, and, to ensure their continued meetings, he made all kinds of promises. As they lay entwined by the Shag Brook, in the setting sun, he would create such stories of the life he would have with his future wife. She knew the hardships that she could expect as a yeoman's wife, and she wanted more than that. So she gave in easily to the ideas of the young man.

As young men do, he wanted more from her than chaste gestures. He felt sure that she would share his desires, and boldly suggested that they share their love in a different way. He was stunned by her response. To her this was an improper suggestion and she was shocked beyond all measure. It was a different world to the one we know today, and even for all her time with him and shared confidences, his proposal outside of marriage was beyond belief.

Her heart gave way and she died instantly of trauma. He held her in his arms as the light went out of her eyes. Suddenly he realised how much he truly loved her, and was full of remorse for having treated her so disrespectfully. He took his knife and plunged it into his heart, watching the blood trickle away as he held her, waiting to be reunited in death.

They were found the next day, still entwined. The stone by the Shag Brook where they had rested was now covered in blood. The bodies were taken away and given a Christian burial. Soon the rains came and washed the stone and filled the brook. But for some reason, the stone seemed to be bleeding itself, flowing into the brook's pure water. Some people said it was to remind people of the hardness of Wickedness and the virtues of Innocence. It continued to bleed for a long, long time.

The soul of the young woman was still traumatised, and was not able to pass over. She was said to wait at the bleeding stone for many a year. People would see her in the darkness, sitting on the stone. Some say that she was waiting for her lover to return for her; some say that she was watching out for other young women who might lose their good name. She became known as the White Lady.

Horses were very sensitive to her presence. In 1800, a tradesman was driving his four horses with a cart laden with corn. The sun was just about to set and the tradesman was keen to get home. However, the horses stopped at the stone and the bridge, refusing to go any further. It didn't matter how many times the tradesman tried his whip, they would not move. Have you ever seen a horse tremble with fear? They put their ears back, they sweat, and their limbs and body shake uncontrollably. In the end, the tradesman unharnessed the horses and took them away from the stone, until they stopped trembling. At daybreak he went to retrieve his cart. Nothing was disturbed, and the horses were easily harnessed to the cart. They went over the bridge without a hint of worry or anxiety.

In 1900 Francis Henry Beaumont, Lord of the Manor, wrote to the *Surrey Magazine* to say that when the Shag Brook was arched over, he had the bleeding stone moved into his garden at the Manor. No one reported seeing the White Lady again. Her dignity had been restored and she was at peace.

Today, the road has been developed and the arch bridge has become part of the A25. There is a garden centre there now, and the Shag Brook runs through a culvert under the car park.

The Buckland Shag

The bleeding stone holds another story or two. Some say it all stems from the wickedness of the young man. Just occasionally, without any rhyme or reason, a 'fearsome four footed beast, like

an ape with a shaggy coat' squats on the bleeding stone at midnight and waits. Some people call it the Buckland Hag or the Buckland Shag.

If by chance you have been quaffing a drink or two at the local hostelry in or around Reigate (there are quite a few), and perhaps make your way a little unsteadily down the road, be warned! The Buckland Shag might appear in front of you.

One jovial drinker, having enjoyed a drink or two too many, proposed to cross the road at midnight to scare off the Shag. It was a beautiful moonlit night, and, as he braced himself, a dark shadow appeared on top of the stone and came tumbling towards him. He gave it a hearty blow with his hawthorn walking stick, then turned and ran as fast as his feet would take him. The shag pursued him all the way home, until he got inside his own front door and collapsed on the floor, where he slept until the morning, his hawthorn stick still clutched in his hand.

Some people say that the Buckland Shag is not a beast but the Devil, amusing himself with dancing. Sometimes he appears in the shape of a donkey or a dog. One old fellow, bolder than his neighbours, took a pitchfork to the Devil. Perhaps to get his own back? But that didn't stop the Devil from dancing!

❧

The people at the garden centre have no business with either the Devil or the Buckland Shag. Very sensibly, they close at 6 p.m., so no one takes the risk of meeting any strange entities at midnight!

TWENTY-EIGHT

THE ANCHORESS
OF SHERE

Taking holy orders is a sincere and devout way of expressing spiritual love and devotion. For many men and women who had no funds or influence, it was the only way they could advance themselves from being a commoner to becoming a respected part of the community. For those who rose to the abbot or abbess role, it was the equivalent of being a chief executive in a modern business, and certainly for many women it was the only way they were able to demonstrate their managerial skills without the undue influence of a man. For others it was a way of avoiding family conflict and trouble.

❦

Christine, daughter of William the carpenter, was a bright girl with a secret. She was enamoured of a young man in her village of Shere. Nothing had been said between them. Nothing had been consummated. She just looked wistfully from afar, and hoped and desired that he might respond in some way. Her father knew nothing of this, and he would have berated her if he knew. He already had plans for his daughter to marry the son of one of his friends. The marriage would suit both families well, and improve their business. Alas, Christine was not interested in this boy; she resented her father's plans and was always looking to the other side of the village for a glimpse of happiness.

There came a day when she couldn't see her favoured young man in the village, and, after several days, she asked of his whereabouts. She was astonished to be told that he had gone to sea. The news hung over her like a veil. She tortured herself that she should have said a word, or made her feelings known – then he might have had a reason to stay. Worse, word soon came to the village that the young man had drowned at sea on his first ship. Now she was bereft, with no one to share her grief.

Her father had no knowledge of his daughter's true feelings, and he wanted to finalise the wedding between the two families in the village. Christine, however, could not bear to marry anyone. The only way she could escape was to dedicate herself to the Church. There were few choices open to her. To become a novice at a convent and withdraw entirely from the world, or become an anchoress, remaining in the community. She would be walled up in the local church, where she could share her devotions to God, and say her prayers for the souls of the departed and for her sins.

Maybe, at the back of her mind, she knew the stories of young men who returned from sea, long after they were reported dead. Maybe she hoped against hope that the young man might come home again. If she was in a convent, then she might never get to hear of his return, but if she was in the community, surely she would. In any case she did not want to marry, and her devotions to God were honourable.

She applied to the Bishop of Winchester to be enclosed, so that she might lead a pious life. Such a request was unusual, and the bishop was very cautious. He ordered a formal inquiry, to test Christine's resolve and understanding of the undertaking she was to make. As an anchoress she would have to experience a strict life. She would be 'anchored under a church like an anchor under the side of the ship'.

After much discussion and questioning, Christine's devotion to the calling was confirmed. Her father was astonished at his daughter's vocation, and urged her to reconsider. After all, he needed grandchildren to look after him in his old age. But she was firm.

The anchorage was built on the side of the church: a small cell containing three windows. One of them was the squint which opened into the church so that she could take part in the church services and take the Holy Communion. The second window was used to pass food into her cell, and for her to pass out a chamber pot. The third window allowed people to come and seek her wisdom, advice and prayers. In her room was a bed, a crucifix and a small altar.

The day of her enclosure came too quickly for her father. She fasted and made confession, and then kept vigil during the night in the church. They held a Mass, where she lay prostrate on the ground. Finally there was a procession of the whole congregation from the church. The enclosure ceremony was held. Christine shivered with anticipation. Relief at escaping an unwanted marriage; excitement at being able to devote herself to her faith. And maybe a fleeting thought that this could preserve her until a day came when someone might come back from the sea. …

She stepped into the cell in her plain dress, black headdress and veil. For the winter months she had a thick blanket to keep out the cold. As she stood there, parts of the burial service were read aloud. In the eyes of the Church, she was now 'dead to the sinful earthly world, but alive to the eternal salvation of heaven'. The stones were then put into the doorway and she was sealed in.

For two years she lived in that cell, saying prayers and devotions. People asked her to pray for them, and intercede on their behalf with God. They brought her food in exchange for these services. Some came to ask advice from this holy woman. Sometimes her father came to see her, and wept as he talked of the lost opportunities for his family and business. Christine dreaded his visits, but also took them as affirmation that her decision to withdraw from the world was correct.

Two years passed. The spring and summer were fine enough, but the winter was bitterly cold, and she had to beg for further garments to keep out the cold of the day, and the deeper cold of the night. Her devotions to God sustained her, but it was becoming more difficult. She was a young woman. How many years would she have to endure this? These thoughts crossed her mind but she would deny them, and prostrate herself in her cell to remove the Devil's temptation.

In the spring a young lass came to Christine to ask for her advice. The son of a neighbour had newly returned from the sea, and the lass wanted to know if it was sinful to ask for prayers that the young man might notice and court her. As they were speaking, Christine suddenly realised that this was the young man she had desired, for whom she had kept herself pure.

Her days and nights were now tormenting her. All the thoughts and feelings she had turned aside in her devotions to God, she now found focused on the young man. She found herself playing and plying at the mortar around the stones that had enclosed her. She told herself that if the stones moved, it was God's will that she should leave the anchorage and find happiness elsewhere.

Over time she worked the mortar loose, until one day she was able to push the stones out and walk free. At first she found herself quite dizzy. She had been in a confined space for so long, that to see beyond 10ft meant that her eyes had to constantly readjust. She was also scared. She had told no one of her plans, believing that to mention it to just one person would make it a conspiracy rather than the hand of God. But where was she to go? Sleeping under the hedge was viable in spring, and no worse

than sleeping in the anchorage. But this was the autumn, and winter was on its way.

She spent two days at the edge of the village, avoiding anyone who came her way. She knew that her disappearance must have been discovered, and that her position was compromised. She could not return to her father's house. She would have to present herself to the young man. Surely he would see the depth of her love in her devotion to God and to him? How could he fail to love her in return?

She washed and cleaned herself. Her hair was matted from her own self-neglect. She approached the village, heading to the house where she believed the young man was staying. She called to him softly, but he did not hear her. She was unsure what to do – and then she saw the young lass walking down the path. Christine hid as the girl passed the house. As she did, the door opened and a man's voice called out to her. The lass smiled and preened herself, delighting in the attention of the young man. He strode out of the house and put his arm around her waist.

'Are you so long away from home, that you have forgotten your manners with a young lady?' she laughed.

The young man also laughed, then scooped her chin and briefly kissed her cheek, saying, 'I have not forgotten any manners.'

With that he took her hand and pulled her with him along the path, past Christine, who turned into the wall, as though hiding from them both.

'Why, Christine, is that you? We have all been so worried about you. What divine intervention brings you here?' asked the young lass.

Christine turned towards them and her face fell. This was not the young man she had waited for. This was a stranger. She had never seen him before. She turned and fled into the woods and lived rough for several weeks, oblivious to the calls and cries of concerned villagers, searching for her. With winter coming and no shelter, starved and almost on the point of death, she went to her father's house. He was angry to see her. He had felt disappointed when she refused the marriage he proposed, and now he felt dishonoured that she had broken her vows and left the anchorage. His feelings were mixed and initially he shunned Christine, turning her from his door. But she begged and pleaded, asking for his forgiveness, and he took her in.

It took several months for Christine to regain her strength. She told no one of her indiscretion, saying only that the stones had been moved by God's hand, and that she had felt bound to re-enter the word at his command. She had lost respect from the community and her father still wanted her to marry. She missed the quietness and solitude of her cell, and the many hours she had spent in contemplation and devotion. There was only one way forward – to reapply to be enclosed, to return to that life of prayer.

The Bishop of Winchester reluctantly agreed to her enclosure, but advised that she should return to her cell within four months or she would be excommunicated from the Church. The local priests were further advised that once Christine was reinstated in the anchorage, they should give her a penance to perform in proportion to her sin.

The door was opened. Christine could return. No one knew of her indiscretion; her fall from grace for the memory of a dead man.

Did she take up that place, or did she risk excommunication? There is no record, but the stigma of excommunication was so great that it is most likely she returned. And so we will leave her in her cell, gathering wisdom about the frailty of the human heart, and how easy it is to deceive ourselves, and learning the solace of devotion, prayer and reflection.

If you visit the church in Shere, you can see the outline of her anchorage on the outside of the church, and the squint inside where she would have received Holy Communion. On the walls inside you can also see the documents that refer to the permission for her enclosure.

TWENTY NINE

THE LEGEND OF STEPHAN LANGTON

(RETOLD FROM MARTIN TUPPER)

When I first came to Surrey and told people I was a storyteller, the story that everyone was eager to tell me was of the Silent Pool. Some said a local duke chased a chaste maid into the pool, where she drowned to save her honour. Some said that King John was the culprit, and that he left his hat behind. But local historians will tell you that the tale did not exist before the intervention of Martin Tupper. He was an English poet, of considerable fame – especially in America – although there were mixed views about the quality of his writing. He was bitterly disappointed that Tennyson was appointed Poet Laureate in 1850, and his literary career began to decline.

He lived in Albury, and hoped that his fortunes would be revived by writing a historical novel about the landscape of the Surrey Hills, where he would draw on local legends and folklore, as well as celebrating the countryside which he loved. He based it around Stephan Langton, who was allegedly born in Friday Street and who eventually went on to become Archbishop of Canterbury and an instigator of the Magna Carta, signed at Runnymede in Surrey. Many of the pieces of stories he used are now 'known to be an old, old story', although there is little evidence that the stories were known before he included them in his history of Stephan Langton.

Martin Tupper started writing the Stephan Langton story on 26 November 1857 and finished on 2 January 1858. I humbly offer you a broad outline of his glorious work, which has wormed its way into local legends and traditions.

How the Seeds of the Magna Carta were Sown

Stephan and Simon Langton were born on the same day in Friday Street. Their father followed the local lord to the Crusades under King Richard, but he was gone so long that he was assumed dead. Their mother took the two boys to her sister's home in the West Country. When their singing attracted the attention of local monks, they were offered a full education in return for positions in the choir. But when their voices broke, and neither boy was interested in the Church, the education finished.

Stephan and his mother returned to Friday Street, to his father's family – and his cousin, the fair Alice. On the May Day celebrations of 1186, Alice was appointed the May Queen, and Stephan's heart was full of love for her.

When the sun went down, Alice and Stephan went into the woods, as did all the other young people. He had a special question for her, and he had a fair idea of her response. They walked down to Collyers Hanger. Although they talked of marriage, she wanted to wait because her mother was ill. So instead she gave Stephan the chaplet of flowers she had worn on her head as May Queen. 'Shall I read you the language of flowers?' she asked him. 'There will be many more tears than smiles in life, I believe, and we must expect our troubles, dearest.'

Stephan looked at the chaplet. It was made from floss silk, with six flower stars, each consisting of five flowers around a rose. He knew well the language of flowers. Anemone for patience; pansy for remembrance; violet for faithfulness; cowslip for sorrow; and lily of the valley for the happiness to come. The red rose for true love.

'No,' said Stephan. 'Don't speak so sadly. This posy should be full of brighter thoughts. I shall wear it around my arm, like this, as your own knight.'

In their passion for each other they did not notice riders approaching – until Stephan was pushed aside, and rough hands reached for Alice. She would make a fine gift for the riders' lord! Stephan tried to stop them but he was knocked out and left for dead, oblivious to Alice's screams.

Stephan was found by old Hal, the woodsman, who had also known his father. From Stephan's description, Hal surmised that the riders must be Prince John's men, staying at Tangley Manor. The two of them struggled through the dark woods and over the marshes to rescue Alice. Once there, Hal distracted the guards while Stephan sneaked in. He could hear Alice's cries, and set light to the sheaves of dry rushes on the floor to provide a distraction.

Stephan burst into the room where Prince John was force-feeding wine to Alice. Using a fire brand, Stephan cleared a circle about him; but Prince John and his knights managed to flee. Alice fainted and, as Stephan tried to comfort her, her clothes caught fire. Stephan carried her out of the blazing inferno, as far as he could, and then laid her down on the marshy ground. To his despair he found she was so badly burned that she was dead. He decided that the best thing to do was to take her to the chapel of St Martha's, and leave her there. Her body and soul would have sanctuary there, and the protection of the Church.

It was almost dawn when he carried her over the threshold, and laid her on the altar steps. He caressed her cold white face, with the red burns etched in to scar her beauty. At that moment he vowed

he would live only to avenge her death, and to stand against the wickedness of Prince John. Tupper says Stephan vowed to 'wear Alice's Chaplet on his arm' and 'free England for ever from the tyranny of kings and recover for the people their ancient liberties'.

Stephan knew that within the Church, a low-born man such as himself could rise up to become the equal of kings. He had the education and training from the monks and knew that he could do it. So he went to nearby Newark Abbey and became a monk. On the way he passed a group of Black Augustinian monks who were going to St Martha's, and Stephan's conscience rested easy, knowing that Alice's body would soon be found and all the burial rites would be performed.

At Newark Abbey, Stephan saw the Abbot and revealed all to him. In sympathy, the Abbot told him that as soon as he was accepted into their order, Stephan could be the first monk at St Martha's. But first he must take holy orders.

The day dawned when Stephan was taken to the chancel at St Martha's. He was to be initiated there, and then he would perform the sacraments to consecrate the chancel in memory of St Thomas à Becket. The convent at nearby St Catherine's had a new novice, and it was arranged that Stephan would hear her vows.

Stephan was initiated and the consecration was made. The young novice nun was brought forward on a litter and it was clear that she had been badly injured. When she raised her veil to take the Communion and looked up at Stephan, he realised that he was looking at the badly burned face of his beloved Alice. She was alive! She had been found by the Black Augustinian monks and taken to St Catherine's Nunnery for recovery. Convinced that Stephan had died, she had decided to take the nun's veil. And now they had both taken vows of celibacy and devotion to God, which in those days was irrevocable. Terrible was the misery of the two, when taken back to their holy homes, to realise that their true love still lived but they could never be together.

If you stand at St Martha's Hill you can still see the priory of St Catherine, and the same the other way. How many times must these two lovers have looked through the windows of their holy commitment, and wondered how life might have been. Stephan wept in despair and rage, and vowed that 'the life of sister Alice [would] stimulate him yet more resolutely to the great achievement of liberty for his downtrodden people … this was not a vow of private vengeance but of patriotic help to wretched England'.

Time passed. Many people sought solace and comfort from the monk on the hill, as they passed St Martha's on the Pilgrims' Way. Most keenly he would listen to barons and serfs, talking of their oppression and the miseries brought in by the Norman kings. And most keenly the barons and serfs would listen to this monk. With careful words, gentle questioning, and sharing of experiences, he became known for scattering seeds of thought that men did not dare to voice for themselves; but now, with encouragement, those seeds 'were sown in the land with hope and strivings after freedom'.

THE LEGEND OF THE SILENT POOL

Old Hal lived with his family in the woods. His wife had died and he was reliant on his eldest daughter Emma and his son Tetbert to look after the younger children. Emma had grown into a beautiful young woman with ruddy cheeks and coal-black hair. Many a wandering minstrel, a lingering pedlar, or a string of packhorses had taken a diversion through the woods purely to be served a drink of water by the young woman at Hal's well. Rumours of her beauty finally reached the ears of Prince John's 'parasitical panderers', and they came to hunt in the woods. After stopping for some water, they left with sly grins on their faces.

Close by was the Shirebourne pool: a small lake hidden among the box bushes, holly trees and other evergreens. This was filled with deep, clear water, 'a mirror to the speck of heaven above'. Trees arched over the top, and the pool had gently shelving sides – the middle dropping sharply into 20ft of water.

In such a quiet, secluded place, young Emma would come to bathe on a hot afternoon. And it was such a hot afternoon that Hal was visited by three young gentlemen. Two of them seemed familiar, but they expressed great interest in his woodwork, and, sensing the possibility of making some money, he was quick to pay them attention. Alas, he didn't pay attention to the third young gentleman, who wore crimson and gold, and a hat with a red feather and a jewelled coronet clasp.

And this was no gentlemen. This was Prince John.

With a sneer, the third man turned away and headed off to the Shirebourne pool. Tetbert watched him leave, and, fearing for his sister's safety, followed on foot as fast as he could.

Emma had undressed and was making her way into the pool when the third rider approached. She grabbed a branch hanging over the pool, hoping that the rider would pass by without seeing her. But he laughed, and encouraged his horse into the water. Emma now realised that she was the subject of his evil intentions. She was in danger! Holding on to the bough, she moved into the centre of the pool. Concentrating hard on the whereabouts of the horseman, she did not notice that she had passed over the shelf —until she lost her footing, and in her panic let go of the bough. Now she was out of her depth, imploring for help. The dark rider pulled up his horse. He could see it was too deep for him. He started to wring out his wet clothes, impervious to the cries and struggles of the young woman.

Tetbert arrived, out of breath; he saw the flailing hands of his sister breaking the water's surface in a last struggle. 'What have you done to her?' he snarled, and then made his way into the water, diving to reach his sister. He caught hold of her and tried to bring her to the surface, but she was caught by a branch. He refused to let her go. They struggled in the water until, held in each other's arms, they both drowned.

The dark rider returned to Hal's house, called to his friends, and they left laughing. Hal was confused, and then became worried when Emma and Tetbert did not appear. He suddenly realised the direction the dark rider had come from, and he sped through the forest to the pool. Everything there was silent. The birds did not sing. There was not even a breeze to ripple the water's surface.

Through the still waters he could see the bodies of his two eldest children, clasped together, at the bottom of the deepest part of that silent pool. As he cast around for something to reach them, he found the hat with a red feather and the jewelled coronet clasp, and realised that the dark rider had been Prince John.

Hal's neighbours came to help retrieve his dead children, and Hal took the hat to Stephan Langton. Tupper records: 'This was the ordeal of persecuted innocence by water, even as Stephan's own had been by fire. It was another victim of that same bad prince who anon was to be demonstrated the very King-curse of England.'

Stephan led the burial service, but seethed in his own heart. In the years since he had become a monk, listened to the stories shared on the Pilgrims' Way, and shared his counsel, Stephan Langton had become known to Prince John as an obnoxious monk, who should be dealt with. Stephan was not to be stopped, and he recounted the story of the Silent Pool to all who came that way. The Abbot of Newark was sent a summons by Prince John to 'give up the incendiary monk who was exciting our good lieges to rebellion on the highway between Winchester and Canterbury'. The Abbot had no option but to obey the royal imperative; but he sent Stephan a warning, so that by the time the soldiers arrived, Stephan was long gone.

Before departing, Stephan had asked his friend Baron Fitzwalter to help Hal seek justice. A plan was devised to enable Hal to 'return' the cap to its rightful owner. Prince John was holding court at Guildford Castle, and Hal, in a suitable disguise, petitioned to ask for justice in a case of murder. John, sensing an opportunity to become more popular with the barons present and to show his authority, asked to hear the story. Told without mention of the culprit's identity, Hal's story created a muttering within the court. All were shocked by the ruthlessness of the perpetrator.

'Yes,' declared John, 'there was murder here. You shall have justice.'

'The murderer,' said Hal, 'left his hat upon the fatal scene, and I have vowed to return it to him, face to face.' Hal threw the hat down in front of Prince John. There was a gasp, as all recognised the insignia of John.

'Treason!' cried one of John's cronies. The guards looked set to arrest Hal.

In the room were a great number of the barons who despaired of their prince. They were now presented with proof of John's culpability. Baron Fitzwalter stood forward, unsheathed his sword and raised it high. John was now apprehensive. Fitzwalter called out: 'Let all who love England follow me!' He turned and left the room, followed by many of the barons who were disgusted at John's behaviour. In the confusion, Hal slipped away.

And so began an association of barons dissatisfied with the rule of John.

THE FLIGHT OF STEPHAN LANGTON, AIDED BY ROBIN HOOD

John responded by giving his cronies permission to put together their own armies as their bodyguards. He was determined to never again feel threatened – but effectively he created a licence for bands of robbers to roam under the patronage of his favoured barons. Tupper describes the land and the people as being torn apart by the ruthlessness of these robbers:

> People were made to make enforced contributions, their land was abandoned, and few would sow a harvest that he had little hope to reap ... The whole land was full of ruin, misery, brigandage and desolation. To the people it didn't matter whether monarch or aristocrat were uppermost, in either event they were trodden on.

Tupper claims that Robert Fitz-Otho, Earl of Huntingdon, gave up his title and estates to be King of the Forests – to be known as Robin Hood. He became 'a free independent link between the oppressed people and their tyrannical rulers: always befriending the poor, helping the wronged to his right, the constant rescuer, and refuge of imperilled womanhood, whether maid, wife or widow'.

Robin Hood's forest wife was Matilda Fitzwalter (later known as Marion), daughter of Baron Fitzwalter, who had fled into the forest to escape the attentions of Prince John. They didn't just stay in the North, in Yorkshire or Nottingham, but went wherever there was injustice to the poor. And Robin Hood had been in disguise outside the hall when Fitzwalter had raised his sword high, calling to other barons to show their disgust at John.

∞∞

When Stephan was on the run, evading Prince John's men, he remembered taking confession from one of Robin Hood's men, who had talked of meeting Robin at the druid yew. Taking a gamble that they were still there, Stephan travelled down the old lane to Albury, and went north of Farlee to the druids' grove. There, at the place we now know as Newlands Corner, he spotted a thin line of blue smoke coming from a yew circle.

He made his way there. Robin's men found him and took him to their leader, and Stephan asked for his protection. Marion was sympathetic to Stephan, and Stephan found himself opening his heart to her of the love he had felt for Alice all these years. He asked her to send a message to Alice that he was leaving the country, but to let her know that he always wore the chaplet of flowers next to his heart.

As all the highways and byways were being watched, the only safe passage was through the forest. Robin volunteered to take Stephan himself, as he 'had some business with the Archbishop of Canterbury'. It took four days to travel to Dover, and in that time Stephan and Robin spoke a great deal about their mutual dissatisfaction with Prince John. Stephan was determined to build up his links with the barons, and Robin provided the ideal network for the nobles and common people to come together against Prince John. It was paramount to both Robin and Stephan that English men became freemen.

Disguised as a fisherman and his wife, they entered Dover. Arrangements were made for Stephan (or rather, the 'fisherman's wife') to travel to France on a herring boat. Arriving in Calais, Stephan took off his disguise and became a young monk, although he did not use his own name. Calais was still under the authority of the English king, so it was not safe for him to reveal his true identity.

Alice, in the meantime, lived solely in the convent. Disfigured and disabled, she was only able to move about on the litter when carried by other nuns. She listened to the nuns talk of Father Langton, a handsome but melancholy man. Her heart leapt every time she heard his name, and she turned a yearning eye towards St Martha's.

Word then came to Alice that her mother was dying. The nuns agreed to take Alice to see her. They would pass St Martha's. Her heart beat strongly – perhaps she would catch a glimpse of Stephan! But when they passed by, Alice learnt that he had fled. She had missed him by half a day.

Her mother died and she returned to the convent. On the way they passed by Hal's cottage. He recognised her, and she asked him to keep her informed of any news of Stephan's whereabouts. Then she received a letter from Maid Marion, which told her all of Stephan's news, and how much he still loved her. Alice asked Hal to find Stephan and look after him, and to take him a lock of her hair. In turn, Hal found Maid Marion and asked for her help in finding Stephan.

Hal went to Dover and then to Calais. His enquiries led him to Rouen, where he found Stephan, now known as Frere Antoine – a monk well respected for his unceasing charity. Pleased to see him, and overwhelmed by the news from both Alice and Marion, Stephan invited Hal to work with him as his valet and confidant.

And so began Hal's work as a courier between Stephan, Robin Hood, and the increasing network of dissatisfied barons on the English shore.

HOW A PIECE OF THE HOLY CROSS CAME TO SURREY

Hal was in the French market at Rouen when he saw an old palmer – a pilgrim with his scallop shell – begging for alms. Amongst the hustle and bustle of the market, Hal was astonished to hear, 'Westone and wodetone. How now neighbour Hal.' The palmer was revealed to be Stephan's father, back from the Crusades; a cripple slowly begging his way home. Alive, but sorely injured.

Astonished to learn that his son, Stephan, was now the Public Praelector in Rouen, the palmer promised that he had a gift of great magnitude – a piece of the True Cross itself. He revealed that, during the battle for Jerusalem, he had stumbled into the room where the True Cross was kept. He was attacked from behind and fell, hitting his jaw on the Cross so hard that a lump fell into his mouth. Losing consciousness, he came to and found that he had been left for dead, and the True Cross had been taken by the infidel army and destroyed. The only remaining relic of the True Cross was the portion in his mouth. This, he gave to Stephan.

Now Stephan saw a way of gaining access to kings and popes. Affidavits were made, notaries visited, and the relic was broken into seven parts, each with a copy of the letter confirming it to be a piece of the True Cross. One piece was given back to his father, and another to the Abbot of Rouen for all the help he had given Stephan. But in making the affidavits, Stephan's true name had been told, and now he had to flee English-held Rouen and seek safety in Paris in the court of the French king. The old man was sent to England with Hal, along with letters to the barons – and a special letter to Alice, along with a piece of the True Cross.

King Philip of France welcomed Stephan; for one thing, he was an antagonist of King John, and for another thing, the meeting was sweetened by the gift of a piece of the True Cross. Prince Arthur, rightful heir to the throne of England, was at the time living in the court of King Philip, along with his mother, Constance of Bretagne. Prince Arthur's father Jeffrey would have been the next in line, but he had died. As Arthur was a babe when King Richard himself died, John had claimed the crown. Stephan swore allegiance to the rightful King of England. Philip was pleased to have a powerful ally in Stephan, especially with his network of contacts. Stephan was made a canon of Paris and a dean of Rheims. His rise in the Church had begun.

In England, Hal delivered the coded letters and the package to Alice. The Abbess had just died, and surely the candidate who had a portion of the True Cross would be triumphant? In 1203, at the age of thirty-four, Alice, who had danced as May Queen aged seventeen, was proclaimed Abbess.

⟨⟩

Now, I have to say that Tupper includes several subplots here, including an Alice lookalike and Stephan's twin brother — who seems to have disappeared from the story for a good long while — but I'll leave all that for you to discover when you read Tupper's writings, as it does not affect our main story!

⟨⟩

One subplot I must tell you is that Arthur, rightful heir to the English throne, had tried to claim the English lands in France as his own. John had challenged him, and their armies fought. Arthur was captured by John, and, as he would not relinquish his claim to the throne, John had him sent to the prison at Rouen, where sadly he died. History is not clear about what happened, but Tupper tells us that Hal witnessed two men take a young man out in a boat on the Seine, cut off his head, and throw the body into the river. Hal recognised the young man as Arthur, and the two men as John's men. Hal told Stephan, who told King Philip.

This all played into Philip's hands. 'Indignant' at a royal death, he proclaimed that 'John of England, Duke of Normandy, be summoned to the court of Philip Augustus, King of France, to answer for the murder of the son of his elder brother.'

Of course, John took no notice, so a hearing was held in his absence. He was found guilty and all his lands in France were declared forfeit to the Crown of France, which happened to be Philip! Only Rouen resisted, whilst all the other territories welcomed the French king. Rouen soon fell and only the islands of Guernsey, Jersey, Alderney and Sark remained of the French territories under the English Crown.

Stephan's influence was now soaring, and he decided to go to Rome to get help for England's sake. He planned that the fifth piece of the True Cross would be given to the Pope.

THE BARONS MEET AT REIGATE CAVES

Word came from England that the tyranny of John was bringing the country to the edge of starvation. Under forest law, the people were deprived of their right to catch even wild ducks, so in hard times the poor could not fall back on the land to get them through. The barons met secretly in the caves at Reigate, and determined that somehow they would overthrow John. They sent messages to Stephan, asking him to return and take the lead in the battle, even though he had not been in the land for ten years.

But Stephan was playing the long game. He was installed at the Pope's palace, and he waited while the Pope pondered how best to thank the man who had just brought him the wonder of a piece of the True Cross.

It so happened that in England the Archbishop of Canterbury had just died. The monks of Canterbury wanted to appoint one of their own brothers to the position, but John had his eye on his crony, the Bishop of Norwich. Fearful of John's response if they said no to his candidate, the monks of Canterbury decided that they would ask the Pope to decide. After all, who had the higher authority in the Church?

The Pope was amused. He saw a chance to humble both the English king and the English clergy, and demonstrate his authority. He declared that he would appoint Stephan to the role – a man of the Church who had experience of the rank, and was furthermore an Englishman. Astonished, the monks offered to pay the Pope 3,000 marks to choose their candidate instead. But the Pope laughed and said, 'Stephan Langton.'

When the news reached England, John recognised the name of the monk who had 'slandered him' on the Pilgrims' Way. He declared Stephan an enemy of the King and stated that he should not set foot on the soil of England. He sent ruffians to Canterbury to dispatch the monks, but they had all fled to Flanders.

The Pope responded by placing England under an interdict, so that all churches were closed, all religious rites were abolished, the dead lay in ditches, and brides married in churchyards. No Mass was said, no prayers were held, and crosses and relics were buried. To the people, this was a disaster.

When John did not respond the Pope excommunicated him, calling him a 'moral leper' and announcing that any man could slay John, and none could help him. Fearful now of everyone about him, John agreed to accept Stephan as Archbishop of Canterbury. But he later recanted. At this point the Pope offered King Philip all of England for the taking, as it 'had no moral leader'. Devastated by this, John capitulated and finally agreed to take Stephan as Archbishop of Canterbury. Philip was furious at being told to stand down – all his plotting so far had got him nowhere!

King John was now compelled to recompense the clergy for the destruction of their property. To do this, he seized all members of the Jewish community and vilely tortured them until they 'gave him their money voluntarily'!

Initially, the barons stood as Englishmen with the King against the Pope, but when John capitulated they stood aside from him. John was desperate for support. The Catholic countries honoured the Pope and would not stand by John. John sent secret emissaries to the Caliph of Granada, offering to convert to the way of Mohammed if they would support him. The Caliph looked at the emissaries. He wanted to know if this conversion was only from King John, or for the whole country. The emissaries knew that John would want them to say the whole country, but in their hearts they could not bring themselves to make this promise, and they confessed it would only be the King. The Caliph waved them away, for without the people's support and conversion the Moors were not interested. A king who promised that must be a madman.

With no support coming from anywhere else in Europe, John conceded all of England and the kingdom of Ireland, plus a tribute of 1,000 marks a year, to the Pope and the Mother Church.

THE RETURN OF STEPHAN AS ARCHBISHOP OF CANTERBURY

The hall in Canterbury was silent as John held out the English crown to Pandulph, the Pope's emissary, and knelt before him. The barons in the hall shook with rage that their sovereignty as a country was such a trifle to John that he would so easily relinquish it. In that moment, the Magna Carta was conceived. The Pope's emissary then crowned John to rule in England on behalf of the Church of Rome.

Stephan was presented as the Lord Archbishop of Canterbury, and John fell at his feet in tears and rage. As Stephan helped him up, he whispered in John's ear, 'Remember Old Tangley?' In that moment, John understood that the scourge of his realm was also that young man he had mercilessly wronged all those years ago. For Stephan, this was the moment he had been waiting for ever since he began his mission to save his country from the injustices of a cruel king.

He planned to travel to London, to the court of King John, but first he wanted to honour the place he had been born, and where he first took holy orders. He travelled through Kent and East Surrey, on the same roads that he had travelled as a fugitive monk dressed as a fisherman's wife. And then he went to the Reigate caverns, where he met the barons, who toasted his return to England to lead them against John. Finally he planned to go to St Martha's, where he had been a monk for so long. A celebration Mass was to be held there, and, of course, the monks of Newark Abbey and the nuns of St Catherine would be invited.

As the day dawned, the monks and nuns made their way to St Martha's. Stephan entered by the Western Arch, remembering the time when he had first stood by the shrine. Next to him was the trembling figure of the Abbess, still in need of assistance to move around. The Communion was held and together they ate of one bread, and drank of one cup. Stephan and Alice looked at one another, eye to eye. In spirit they were ever as one, even as in body they were divided.

After the benediction the nuns and monks began to leave. The Abbess remained at the Communion rail. No one thought anything of it, as she was known for her devotions. Stephan disrobed from his ceremonial clothes, hoping to talk to Alice for the first time in twenty-seven years. He saw her at the Communion rail at her prayers. He knelt beside her, placed his hand on hers, and whispered, 'It is I. Stevie.'

But Alice could make no answer. In her joy and delight at seeing Stephan again, and having shared Communion with him, her heart made one last leap for joy, and with that she died. For her it was better to have died than to live a melancholy life, divorced from the man she loved who was now so close to her.

Stephan shook with rage and grief for his lost love, who was dead thanks to a man not fit to be king. The nuns came and took their Abbess's body away. Stephan sent orders to a mason in Guildford to set a stone each side of the chancel at St Martha's, flush to the floor. Alice's funeral was held at St Martha's, overseen by Stephan. She was laid to eternal rest in the chancel by the weeping nuns.

But there was more to be done. Stephan met the barons at the Reigate caves, and, on 25 August 1213, Stephan read out the Charter of Liberties first set out by King Henry I 100 years earlier. It was enshrined in English law, and they drew on it to confirm their rights. The Magna Carta was drafted in the caves. On Friday 15 June 1215, on the plains of Runnymede, the King was summoned and made to sign the Magna Carta. Faced with such opposition from his barons, John had little choice. The first man to sign it after the King was Stephan Langton. A lifetime's work had finally been achieved.

Stephan continued to campaign and rile a king that showed no compassion or respect for his country. John tried to rescind the Magna Carta, and Civil War broke out. Louis of France tried to invade from the south, and Alexander of Scotland from the north. It took another twelve years for the Magna Carta to be fully implemented. John died in 1216.

Faithful Hal, still by Stephan's side after all these years, was the only one who knew the true cost to Stephan. In the evening, when they sat together, Stephan asked for his body to be laid to rest next to Alice's when he died.

As he was the Archbishop of Canterbury, when he did die, it was arranged that his coffin be taken to Canterbury for burial, with full pomp and ceremony. But Hal, good faithful Hal, arranged for two coffins to be brought from Dorking. One was filled with earth and placed in the grand funeral carriage. The other was discretely removed from the place and taken at night to St Martha's, where the Abbot of Newark conducted a private funeral. The body of Stephan Langton was laid in the chancel next to Alice. United at last in death.

∽∾

This is the story told by Martin Tupper in his celebration of the land-scape and traditions of the Surrey Hills. How much is tradition, how much is true, and how much Martin Tupper made up, I do not know. But I can tell you that in 1829, Richard Thompson wrote 'An historical essay on the Magna Charta of King John'. Here is an extract:

In a communication from the Abbe de la Rue, printed in the Archeologia Vol xiii., page 231, it is stated that in the Duke of Norfolk's library there is a manuscript containing a sermon and two other pieces written by Langton: and that in the course of the Sermon, which is on the holy Virgin, there occurs the following stanza

Fair Alice arose in the morning
And she pot on her vest and made her ready;
Then she went into her bower
And there found five flowerets
Which she made into a chaplet
With the blooming rose
And you will betray god herein
If you do not love me

∼

And throughout the rest of the sermon to the virgin, is a repeated phrase.

This, this is Alice, fair to see
The flower, the lily, this is she.

I will leave you to draw your own conclusions!

THIRTY

A NEW STORY –
OR HOW STORIES
CAME TO BE

This is a story that was developed to show schoolchildren how a folk tale can arise out of a real event. In February 2009, I was trying to get to Peaslake School during a period of heavy snow. Colmans Hill is very steep, and my car kept sliding backwards down it. I met three people who tried to help me, and this story is my thanks to them. The choice of three gifts is an old motif, appearing in The Merchant of Venice *and many older tales.*

It was the second day in February. A very cold day. The snow was thick on the ground and all you could hear was the crunching of snow as the old woman started to walk up Colmans Hill. It's a steep path up to the top, but, once there, in the old days you could see across the valley. Now there is a school there. On the other side, it's a sheer drop down.

Along the path, the old woman was carefully putting one foot in front of the other. On her back was a sack and, if you looked carefully, you could see it was full – and every now and then something moved.

'Alright,' the old woman said, 'I'm getting there. When I get to the top of the hill, then I can let you go free'.

The snow was cold and the wind was blowing it upwards, causing it to whip her face. On the side of the road was a young woman, sitting on a bench. The old woman asked, 'Is this the way to the top of Colmans Hill?'

The young woman said, 'Yes, but it's a long way and it's very dangerous. Be careful or you will slip and fall. Why don't you go back down and try another day?'

The old woman shook her head and said, 'I must get to the top of the hill.' On her back something in the sack moved again. The old woman looked inside the bag, 'It's alright,' she whispered, 'I will free you.'

The young woman said, 'If you must go up the hill, keep to the right-hand side. The ice is not so bad there and you are away from the edge.' The old woman thanked her for the advice and she went on her way, up the hill.

It was very steep, and the ice was getting thicker. The old woman slipped and fell to her knees. Ouch! Standing by the side of the road was an old man. 'Are you alright?' he asked. The old woman replied, 'No, I'm not. I have to get to the top of this hill – but I have fallen over and now my knees are hurting!'

The old man came over and very carefully helped the old woman get to her feet. He said, 'It's a long way to the top of the hill and it's very dangerous. Be careful or you will slip and fall. Why don't you go back down and try another day?'

The old woman shook her head. 'It has to be today,' she said.

The old man shook *his* head. Then he went to the side of the road where there was a tree, with snow on its branches. He broke off a branch and then gave it to her. He said, 'If you must go up the hill today, then use this stick.'

The old woman thanked him and continued on her way up the hill. The stick was very good, but she found that every time she put her foot down, she started to slip. Soon she was so scared to move that she became bent over her stick, unable to go anywhere. And she might have stayed there a very long time if a young man hadn't come along the road. 'Are you alright?' he said.

The old woman cried, 'I must get to the top of the hill! But I am scared.'

The young man said, 'Then let me help you.'

And he bent down and put the old woman and her sack on his back. Taking her stick, he made his way slowly up the hill, one step at a time. He made sure he was steady before he took each step. At the top of the hill, he let the old woman off his back. Something in the sack was moving, almost jumping around.

'What's that?' he asked.

The old woman smiled. 'It's stories,' she said. 'All the stories of Surrey, all to warm the cockles of the heart on a cold, snowy day.' With that she opened the sack. 'Have a look.'

Inside the sack were bright lights of different colours – red, yellow, green, blue, gold and silver. And a humming and a muttering – soft and low, loud and high. Suddenly all the lights and noises swirled and moved up out of the sack, and it felt like a warm rush of kisses on the young man's face as they passed into the sky. And as he looked he could see fairies, dragons, winged horses, witches, and even a little devil. Was that a flying pig? Many shapes and figures fluttering about, telling their stories.

The old woman cried, 'Go!' and the rainbow of stories swirled in different directions. The young man tried to catch them but they slipped through his fingers. The sack was empty.

'It's alright,' said the old woman, 'you will get the stories back from the children. But,' she added, 'I must say thank you and give you something in return.' She took out her purse and he could see there were just three coins in it. One gold, one silver, one copper. She put them on her hand. 'With these coins I can give you one blessing. The gold one is for wealth, the silver is for success, and the copper is for love. Which one will you choose?'

The young man looked at each. He could certainly use wealth and he craved success. But he remembered his family and chose the copper coin. 'I choose love'.

With that the old woman laughed and gave him all three. 'Many blessings on you,' she said, 'because with love, both success and wealth will surely follow.'

As they stood there, the sack moved again. The young man bent down to pick it up, and opened it. Inside was a new light and a different kind of murmuring. The old woman laughed again. 'Look,' she said, 'we have created a new story. Will you let this one go free?'

The young man opened the sack, and the story flew up into the air and was away – to be told and retold, just as I have told it to you.

∽

When I was researching stories for this book, I met a woman in a café in Farnham and told her what I was doing. 'Oh,' she said, 'I know a story about stories that my daughter told me.' She then told me a rough outline of this story!

From my mouth to a child's ear; from a child's mouth to a mother's ear; from her mouth to my ear. It had taken just three years to travel back to me.

NOTES ON THE STORIES

1. THE DRAGON OF WEST CLANDON

The original newspaper clipping was in the Gentleman's Magazine of 1796, and is referenced in:

Lane, M., *Surrey Lore and Legend*, 1999
Parker, E., *Highways and Byways in Surrey*, 1921

The background information on the revolt came from this paper:

Jane Austen & the Wars (http://www.theloiterer.org/essays/war-spart1.html)

If you want to find the outline of the dragon in the embankment:

http://www.hows.org.uk/personal/hillfigs/cland/drag.htm

2. ST MARTHA AND THE DRAGON

The story of St Martha can be found in:

de Voragine, J., *The Golden Legend*, 1260
http://www.fordham.edu/halsall/basis/goldenlegend/
GoldenLegend-Volume4.asp#Martha

You can find more information on the Tarasque and the festival by
looking at:

en.wikipedia.org/wiki/Tarasque

3. How the Giant Sisters Learned About Cooperation

The story of the giant sisters is mentioned in:

Dashwood, J.B., *The Thames to the Solent by Canal and Sea*, 1868

Clinch, G. and Kershaw, S.W., *Bygone Surrey*, 1860

Who knows what rhyme might have been used, but 'up scout, walk
out' is the one recorded in Surrey by Steve Roud in 2008, so it's as
good as any to resolve an impasse between giants.

Roud, S., *The Lore of the Playground*, 2010

4. How the Power of a Dream and a Pike Created a Great Man

This story is mentioned in:

Dashwood, J.B., *The Thames to the Solent by Canal and Sea*, 1868

Parker, E., *Highways and Byways in Surrey*, 1921

5. The Fair Maid of Astolat

This story is in:

Malory, Sir Thomas, *Le Morte d'Arthur*

6. Captain Salvin and the Flying Pig

This story is mentioned in:

Parker, E., *Highways and Byways in Surrey*, 1921

Lee, S., *Dictionary of National Biography*

More about Captain Salvin can be found at:

http://www.woodlandsfalconry.com/history-falconry-in-ireland

7. The Treacherous Murder of a Good Man

This well-documented story can be found in:

Parker, E., *Highways and Byways in Surrey*, 1921

Janaway, J., *Surrey Murders*, 1988

S. Baring-Gould used this story at the backdrop to his novel *The Broom-Squire*

8. How the Devil's Jumps and the Devil's Punch Bowl Came To Be

Parker, E., *Highways and Byways in Surrey*, 1921

Simpson, J., *Folklore of Sussex*, 1973

http://www.3counties10k.co.uk

http://www.sussexarch.org.uk/saaf/devil.html

9. Old Mother Ludlam and her Healing Cauldron

There are many references to this tale, and Alexander summarises some of the variants. The tale told here is my version, which has been fashioned from my retelling it in local schools.

Cobbett, W., *Rural Rides*, 1830

Clinch, G. and Kershaw, S.W., *Bygone Surrey*, 1860

Alexander, M., *The Fair Maid of Guildford and Other Surrey Tales*, 1986, 2003

Westwood, J. and Simpson, J., *The Lore of the Land*, 2005

10. The Revenge of William Cobbett

New York Times book review of *William Cobbett: A Biography* by
E. Smith (http://query.nytimes.com/mem/archive-free/pdf?_r=1&
res=9400E6D7153EE63BBC4953DFB4678383669FDE)
Alexander, M., *Tales of Old Surrey*, 1985

11. Mathew Trigg and the Pharisees

The only place I have found this story is in:
Alexander, M., *More Surrey Tales*, 1986

12. The Surrey Puma

The first reference to the Surrey puma is at:
Cobbett, W., *Rural Rides*, 1830

A version of the Chinese myth I based it on is at:
www.messybeast.com/moggycat/chinese.htm

13. Not So Wise Men

The Hermit of Painshill
Parker, E., *Highways and Byways in Surrey*, 1921
Clark, J., 'The King, the Hermit and Lightning', 2009 (Guide
notes at Painshill)

Cocker Nash
Thompson, D., *Change and Tradition in Rural England:
An Anthology of Writings on Country Life*, 1980

14. THE GOLDEN FARMER

Westwood, J. and Simpson, J., *The Lore of the Land*, 2005
A biography of Davies is at:
http://www.berkshirehistory.com/bios/wdavies.html (Edited from
Leslie Stephen's *Dictionary of National Biography*)

15. THE CURFEW BELL SHALL NOT RING TONIGHT

Parker, E., *Highways and Byways in Surrey*, 1921
Alexander, M., *Tales of Old Surrey*, 1985

16. EDWY THE FAIR, AND THE DASTARDLY ST DUNSTAN

Butterworth, H., *ZigZag Journeys in Northern Lands; The Rhine to the Arctic*, 1884
Crake, A.D., *Edwy the Fair or the First Chronicle of Aescendune*, 1853
Chouler, W.H., *Tales of Old Surrey*, 1988

17. THE LOSS OF NONSUCH PALACE

There were many sources available to me, but these were the most helpful:

Lysons, D., *The Environs of London*, Vol. 1: County of Surrey, 1792
Willis, C.S., *A Short History of Ewell and Nonsuch*, 1931
Dent, J., *The Quest for Nonsuch*, 1962
Lister, L., *Nonsuch: Pearl of the Realm*, 1992
The story of the ghosts is at:
http://surrey.greatbritishlife.co.uk/article/surreys-most-haunted-sites--spooky-halloween-stories-10094

18. A Dish Fit for a Queen

'Addington', *The Environs of London*, Vol. 1: County of Surrey, 1792
http://www.british-history.ac.uk/report.aspx?compid=45369
Dugdale, Thomas, *Curiosities of Great Britain: England and Wales Delineated*, Vol. 1, 1835
http://www.gutenberg.org/files/37519/37519-h/37519-h.htm

19. The Mystery of Polly Paine

Fairall, H., *Glorious Godstone*, 1935
Alexander, M., *Tales of Old Surrey*, 1985
The Fancy Free walk for Godstone has some information, but draws mainly on Fairall's book. It is useful for finding the local features. (http://www.fancyfreewalks.org/SurreySouth.html)

20. The Rollicking History of a Pirate and Smuggler

Fairall, H., *Glorious Godstone*, 1935
This includes a chapter called 'Pirate who Died so Far From the Sea [written by a Scout]'. As far as I can find, most of the current stories of John Trenchman derive from this source, and if anyone knows of an earlier source, I'd be delighted to know.
http://www.fancyfreewalks.org/SurreySouth.html

Norton, R., *A study of Criminal Subcultures in Eighteenth-Century England*, and also at: http://rictornorton.co.uk/gu13.htm
This source has a lot of contemporary information on smugglers

21. Rhymes, a Riddle, Poems and a Song!

Sutton for Mutton
Thiselton-Dyer, T.F., *Folklore of Women: As Illustrated by Legendary and Traditionary Tales*, 1905

The Tunning of Elinor Rumming
http://stagingthehenriciancourt.brookes.ac.uk/historicalcontext/
tunning_of_elinor_rumming.html

Riddle on the Letter H
Bright, J.S., *Dorking: A History of the Town*, 1876

The Fairies' Farewell
Written by Richard Corbet

www.britannica.com/EBchecked/topic/1353071/Richard-Corbet
A commentary on the fairy lore he uses is at:
www.wwnorton.com/college/.../27636_17th_U13_Corbet-1-2.pdf

Poor Murdered Woman
Broadwood, L., *English Traditional Songs and Carols*, 1908

22. The Trial of Joan Butts, so-called Witch of Ewell

Burgiss, E., *Strange and Wonderful News from Yowel in Surry*, 1681

An analysis of the above is at:
http://witching.org/brimstone/detail.php?mode=shorttitle&short
itle=13

There is a lot of information on the local history site:
http://www.epsomandewellhistoryexplorer.org.uk/Witch.html

23. TROUBLESOME BULLBEGGARS

Briggs, K.M., *Encyclopedia of Fairies*, 1976
Simpson, J. and Roud, S., *A Dictionary of English Folklore*, 2000
http://www.housesinwoking.com/Webpage/129/History-of-Horsell

24. THE WILD CHERRY TREE AND THE NUTHATCH

Rhodes, M.B., *Songs and Stories of Ruth Tongue*, 2009

25. THE PHARISEES OF TITSEY WOOD

Leveson-Gower, G., 'Surrey Etymologies – Tandridge Hundred: II',
Surrey Arch., Coll. 6, 1874

26. THE UPSIDE DOWN MAN

The Gentleman's Magazine, June 1800
Simpson, J., 'The Miller's Tomb: Facts, Gossip, and Legend', 2005
Folklore, Vol. 116, No. 2, pp. 189-200

The following is an autobiography by a great-great-nephew of the upside down man, in which he refers to a family story:

de la Billière, Peter, *Looking for Trouble: SAS to Gulf Command: the Autobiography*, 1995

27. THE BUCKLAND BLEEDING STONE

The Gentleman's Magazine, December 1827
Soane, G., *New Curiosities of Literature*, 1849
Alexander, M., *Tales of Old Surrey*, 1985

28. The Anchoress of Shere

Alexander, M., *Tales of Old Surrey*, 1985

Details of the life and rules of being an anchoress:
   http://www.middle-ages.org.uk/anchoress.htm

29. The Legend of Stephan Langton

Tupper, Martin, *Stephan Langton: A Tale of the Days of King John*, 1858
David Rose sent me a copy of his article on 'Martin Tupper's myths'
from *Guildford – Our Town*

The poem about Alice can be found in:
   The Antiquary, June 1882 (accessed via: http://www.archive.org/
   stream/antiquary15appegoog/antiquary15appegoog_djvu.txt)
   Thompson, Richard, *An historical essay on the Magna Charta of
   King John* can be found at: http://archive.org/details/historicales-
   sayo00thomuoft

30. A New Story – Or How Stories Came To Be

I made this one up to show how stories can develop from real events

If you enjoyed this book, you may also be interested in…

London Folk Tales
HELEN EAST

London is a world unto itself; an outrageous, quirky and diverse microcosm where all walks of life cross paths – and there are tales whichever way you turn. Here you will find Dick Whittington alongside the patron saint of cobblers, a royal rat rubbing shoulders with the Maid Uncumber, and fish that decide destinies. Revisit old friends and discover new ones in this wonderful selection of London folk tales – as full of unexpected twists as the streets of London itself.

978 0 7524 6185 4

Essex Folk Tales
JAN WILLIAMS

The Essex coastline has endured many bloodthirsty invasions. The spirits of these intruders, and countless others, have oft been reported – not least by smugglers determined to keep intruders away from their secret hideouts. Even more dramatic stories lurk inland: accusations of witchcraft have been screamed around market towns, dragons have terrorised the community, and a violent White Lady has struck at Hadleigh Castle.

978 0 7524 6600 2

Leicestershire & Rutland Folk Tales
LEICESTERSHIRE GUILD OF STORYTELLING

The ancient counties of Leicestershire and Rutland are home to a rich and diverse collection of tales. From epic battles, brave knights and heroic deeds to giants, ghosts and griffins, and with horrors ranging from the fearsome Black Annis who dwells in the Dane Hills to bogeymen who haunt castle ruins, Leicestershire & Rutland Folk Tales brings alive the landscape of the counties' rolling hills and fertile plains.

978 0 7524 8578 2

Visit our website and discover thousands of other History Press books.

www.thehistorypress.co.uk